Reader's Theater Scripts

Improve Fluency, Vocabulary, and Comprehension

TEACHER RECOMMENDED · STANDARDS & RESEARCH BASED

Author

Cathy Mackey Davis, M.Ed.

SHELL EDUCATION

Publishing Credits

Dona Herweck Rice, *Editor-in-Chief*; Lee Aucoin, *Creative Director*; Don Tran, *Print Production Manager*; Conni Medina, M.A.Ed., *Editorial Director*; Jamey Acosta, *Assistant Editor*; Juan Chavolla, *Production Artist*; Corinne Burton, M.S.Ed., *Publisher*

Shell Education
5301 Oceanus Drive
Huntington Beach, CA 92649-1030
http://www.shelleducation.com
ISBN 978-1-4258-0693-4
© 2010 by Shell Educational Publishing, Inc.
Reprinted 2012

Table of Contents

Introduction

The Connection Between Fluency and Reader's Theater

What Is Reader's Theater?

With reader's theater, students use scripts to practice for a performance. The students do not memorize their lines, and costumes and props are minimal, if used at all. The students convey the meaning of the words using their voices; therefore, interpretation of the text becomes the focus of the activity. Reader's theater gives students at all levels the motivation to practice fluency. The U.S. Department of Education's *Put Reading First* (2001) says: "Reader's theater provides readers with a legitimate reason to reread text and to practice fluency. Reader's theater also promotes cooperative interaction with peers and makes the reading task appealing."

What Is Reading Fluency?

Reading fluency is the ability to read quickly and accurately with meaning, while at the same time using vocal expression (to portray feelings and emotions of characters) and proper phrasing (timing, intonation, word emphasis). The fluent reader groups words in meaningful ways that closely resemble spoken language. Fluency is now seen as a direct connection to reading comprehension (Kuhn and Stahl 2000). It bridges the gap between word recognition and reading comprehension.

The National Reading Panel Report (National Institute of Child Health and Human Development 2000) identified five critical factors that are necessary for effective reading instruction. These factors are:

- phonemic awareness
- phonics
- fluency
- vocabulary
- comprehension

Fluency is particularly important for children first learning to read. LaBerge and Samuels (1974) state that readers have a limited amount of attention to focus on reading. Teachers notice this phenomenon when, after listening to a struggling reader, they find that the student cannot explain what he or she has just read. The struggling student has used all available concentration to decode the words and thus fails to grasp the full meaning of the text.

A student who reads fluently processes the text with more comprehension. Timothy Rasinski (1990) found that grouping words into phrases improves comprehension. When the text sounds like natural speech, students are better able to use their own knowledge and experiences to enhance comprehension.

Introduction *(cont.)*

The Connection Between Fluency and Reader's Theater *(cont.)*

How Is Fluency Developed?

Oral reading practice is required for fluency development. Building fluency takes time and develops gradually with practice. A 1979 study by Samuels supports the power of rereading as a fluency builder. In this study, students with learning problems were asked to read a passage several times. Each time the students reread the selection, their reading rate, accuracy, and comprehension increased. The most surprising finding in Samuels's study is that these students also improved on initial readings of other passages of equal or greater difficulty. Their increase in fluency transferred to new and unknown passages.

How Can Reader's Theater Develop Fluency?

Each reader's theater script includes parts for several children to read together, therefore facilitating student participation in a limited form of paired reading, another proven fluency strategy. In paired reading, a stronger reader is partnered with a struggling reader. By listening to the fluent reader, the struggling reader learns how voice, expression, and phrasing help to make sense of the words. This strategy also provides a model for the struggling reader and helps him or her to move through the text at an appropriate rate.

Reader's theater is a simple tool that supports multiple aspects of reading and nets significant gains in reading for the students. It is not only effective in developing reading fluency, it is a motivating factor that can transform a class into eager readers. It is one activity within the school day in which struggling readers do not stand out. With teacher support and repeated practice, all students can do the following:

- ➤ read their lines with accuracy and expression
- ➤ gain confidence in their own reading abilities
- ➤ enhance their listening, vocabulary development, decoding, comprehension, and speaking skills

Introduction *(cont.)*

A Note to Teachers from a Working Teacher

 **From the Desk of
Cathy Mackey Davis**

This book can make a teacher's life easier and provide students with beneficial reading activities. After more than 20 years as an elementary teacher, I thought I'd seen everything come down the reading pike until I received extensive training on the five components of reading. The concept of direct instruction on fluency both surprised and impressed me.

These reader's theater scripts are designed with classroom management in mind. Each reader's theater has assigned roles for students, enabling the teacher to divide the class into small groups, which can be easily monitored. Students can develop fluency through choral reading, an effective strategy that helps students practice their reader's theater parts.

Each script in this book has its own ready-to-use, teacher-friendly lesson plan. The lesson plans cover three key components of reading: vocabulary, comprehension, and fluency. The discussion questions go beyond the literal understanding of a text in an attempt to raise the students' comprehension levels. Graphic organizers are an important part of the lessons, offering direction and bringing closure to the day's activity.

The scripts can also be an addition to classroom Literacy Work Stations. The teacher can place copies of the scripts in a Drama Station or a Fluency Station. Then students choose their parts and practice with minimal teacher intervention. The discussion questions from the lesson plans can be printed on index cards as a part of the station materials. The graphic organizers from the lessons can be enlarged on poster paper as a culminating activity for the stations.

By its very nature, reader's theater encourages students to reread and to use expression and phrasing to convey the meaning of words. It is an activity that both challenges proficient readers and motivates reluctant readers.

Cathy Mackey Davis, M.Ed.
Third Grade Teacher

Introduction *(cont.)*

Differentiation

Classrooms have evolved into diverse pools of learners—English language learners and students performing above grade level, below grade level, and on grade level. Teachers are expected to meet the diverse needs of all students in one classroom. Differentiation encompasses what is taught, how it is taught, and the products children create to show what they have learned. These categories are often referred to as content, process, and product. Teachers can keep these categories in mind as they plan instruction that will best meet the needs of their students.

Differentiating for Below-Grade-Level Students

Below-grade-level students will need help with complex concepts. They need concrete examples and models to help with comprehension. They may also need extra guidance in developing oral and written language. By receiving extra support and understanding, these students will feel more secure and have greater success.

> - Model fluent reading before asking students to practice on their own.
> - Allocate extra practice time for oral language activities.
> - Allow for kinesthetic (hands-on) activities where appropriate. For example, students may act out the meaning of a vocabulary word.

Differentiating for Above-Grade-Level Students

All students need a firm foundation in the key vocabulary and concepts of the curriculum. Even above-grade-level students may not know much about these words or concepts before a lesson begins. The difference is that they usually learn the concepts quickly. The activities and end products can be adapted appropriately for individual students.

> - Ask students to explain their reasoning for their decisions about phrasing, intonation, and expression.
> - Have students design their own reader's theater scripts.

Differentiating for English Language Learners

Like all learners, English language learners need teachers who have a strong knowledge base and are committed to developing students' language. It is crucial that teachers work carefully to develop English language learners' academic vocabularies. Teachers of English language learners should keep in mind the following important principles:

> - Make use of realia, concrete materials, visuals, pantomime, and other nonlinguistic representations of concepts to make input comprehensible.
> - Ensure that students have ample opportunities for social interactions.
> - Create a nonthreatening atmosphere that encourages students to use their new language.
> - Introduce words in rich contexts that support meaning.
> - Respect and draw on students' backgrounds and experiences and build connections between the known and the new.

Introduction *(cont.)*

How to Use This Book

This book includes 14 reader's theater scripts and grade-level-appropriate lessons. Within each focused lesson you will find suggestions for how to connect the script to a piece of literature and a specific content area; a vocabulary mini-lesson; activities for before, during, and after reading the script; and written and oral response questions.

Literature Connection →

Content Connection →

Vocabulary Activity →

Before the Reader's Theater →

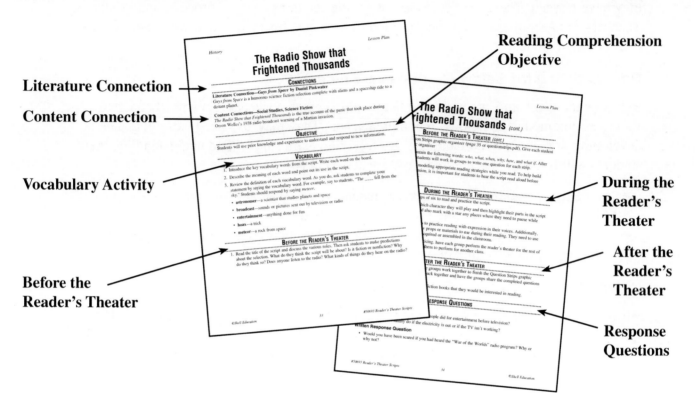

Reading Comprehension Objective

During the Reader's Theater

After the Reader's Theater

Response Questions

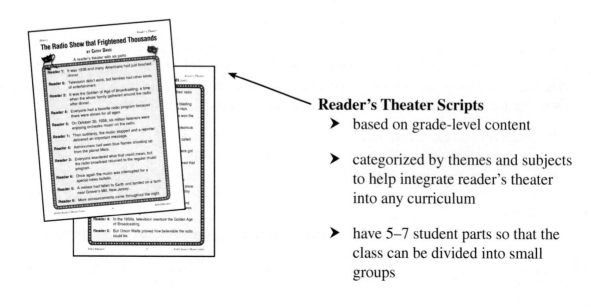

Reader's Theater Scripts

➤ based on grade-level content

➤ categorized by themes and subjects to help integrate reader's theater into any curriculum

➤ have 5–7 student parts so that the class can be divided into small groups

Introduction *(cont.)*

How to Use This Book *(cont.)*

Each lesson introduces a specific graphic organizer. A reproducible copy of each graphic organizer is provided in the lesson. Additionally, a PDF of each graphic organizer is available on the Teacher Resource CD.

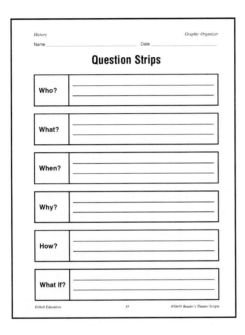

Suggestions for Using and Displaying the Graphic Organizer

➤ **Make a transparency** of the graphic organizer and use it as a model during the lesson.

➤ **Use chart paper** to recreate the graphic organizer. Complete the graphic organizer as you teach the lesson.

➤ **Use the electronic copy** of the graphic organizer from the Teacher Resource CD to project onto the board or an interactive whiteboard.

Contents of the Teacher Resource CD

➤ PDF of each graphic organizer

➤ PDF of each script

➤ The contents of the CD are listed on page 102.

Introduction *(cont.)*

Standards Correlations

Shell Education is committed to producing educational materials that are research and standards based. In this effort, we have correlated all of our products to the academic standards of all 50 states, the District of Columbia, and the Department of Defense Dependent Schools.

How to Find Standards Correlations

To print a customized correlation report of this product for your state, visit our website at **http://www.shelleducation.com** and follow the on-screen directions. If you require assistance in printing correlation reports, please contact Customer Service at 1-877-777-3450.

Purpose and Intent of Standards

The No Child Left Behind legislation mandates that all states adopt academic standards that identify the skills students will learn in kindergarten through grade twelve. While many states had already adopted academic standards prior to NCLB, the legislation set requirements to ensure the standards were detailed and comprehensive.

Standards are designed to focus instruction and guide adoption of curricula. Standards are statements that describe the criteria necessary for students to meet specific academic goals. They define the knowledge, skills, and content students should acquire at each level. Standards are also used to develop standardized tests to evaluate students' academic progress.

Teachers are required to demonstrate how their lessons meet state standards. State standards are used in development of all of our products, so educators can be assured they meet the academic requirements of each state.

McREL Compendium

We use the Mid-continent Research for Education and Learning (McREL) Compendium to create standards correlations. Each year, McREL analyzes state standards and revises the compendium. By following this procedure, McREL is able to produce a general compilation of national standards. Each lesson in this product is based on one or more McREL standards. The chart on the following pages lists each standard taught in this product and the corresponding lessons.

Introduction *(cont.)*

Correlations to Standards

Language Arts Standards	
Lesson Title	**McREL Standard**
Booker T. Washington	Summarizes and paraphrases information in texts (e.g., includes the main idea and significant supporting details of a reading selection).
The Rhyming Author	Uses prior knowledge and experience to understand and respond to new information.
Black Bart the Po8	Summarizes and paraphrases information in texts (e.g., includes the main idea and significant supporting details of a reading selection).
The Radio Show that Frightened Thousands	Uses prior knowledge and experience to understand and respond to new information.
The Dust Bowl	Uses text organizers (e.g., headings, topic and summary sentences, graphic features, typeface, chapter titles) to determine the main ideas and to locate information in a text.
The Story of Basketball	Understands structural patterns or organization in informational texts (e.g., chronological, logical, or sequential order; compare-and-contrast; cause-and-effect; proposition and support).
The Mountain Lion	Uses text organizers (e.g., headings, topic and summary sentences, graphic features, typeface, chapter titles) to determine the main ideas and to locate information in a text.
Learn About Ducks	Summarizes and paraphrases information in texts (e.g., includes the main idea and significant supporting details of a reading selection).
The Mud Puppy	Uses text organizers (e.g., headings, topic and summary sentences, graphic features, typeface, chapter titles) to determine the main ideas and to locate information in a text.
Cool Cow Facts	Makes, confirms, and revises simple predictions about what will be found in a text (e.g., uses prior knowledge and ideas presented in text, illustrations, titles, topic sentences, key words, and foreshadowing clues).
Goldie and the Three Bears	Understands similarities and differences within and among literary works from various genre and cultures (e.g., in terms of settings, character types, events, point of view; role of natural phenomena).
Helping Monkeys	Summarizes and paraphrases information in texts (e.g., includes the main idea and significant supporting details of a reading selection).
Chickenpox	Summarizes and paraphrases information in texts (e.g., includes the main idea and significant supporting details of a reading selection).
The Charreada	Summarizes and paraphrases information in texts (e.g., includes the main idea and significant supporting details of a reading selection).

Introduction *(cont.)*

Correlations to Standards *(cont.)*

Vocabulary Standards	
Lesson Title	**McREL Standard**
All scripts	Uses a variety of context clues to decode unknown words (e.g., draws on earlier reading, reads ahead)
All scripts	Understands level-appropriate reading vocabulary (e.g., synonyms, antonyms, homophones, multi-meaning words).

Fluency Standards	
Lesson Title	**McREL Standard**
All scripts	Uses a variety of nonverbal communication skills (e.g., eye contact, gestures, facial expressions, posture.)
All scripts	Uses a variety of verbal communication skills (e.g., projection, tone, volume, rate, articulation, pace, phrasing).

Introduction (cont.)

Tips on Reader's Theater

By Aaron Shepard

Mumble, mumble,

Stop and stumble.

Pages turn and readers fumble.

If this sounds like a description of your reader's theater efforts, try giving your readers the following tips. First, have your readers follow these instructions—individually or in a group—to prepare their scripts and get familiar with their parts.

Preparing	• Highlight your parts in your copy of the script. Mark only the words you will say—not your character's name or stage directions. • Underline the words that tell about anything you'll need to act out. • Read through your part aloud. If you're a character, think about how that character would sound. How does your character feel? Can you speak as if you were feeling that way? • Stand up and read through the script again. If you're a character, try out faces and movements. Would your character stand or move in a special way? Can you do that?
Rehearsing	• Hold your script at a steady height, but make sure it doesn't hide your face. • Speak with feeling. • S-l-o-w d-o-w-n. Say each syl-la-ble clear-ly. • TALK LOUDLY! You have to be heard in the back row. • While you speak, try to look up often. Don't just look at your script. • The narrators are important even when the audience isn't looking at you. You control the story! Be sure to give the characters enough time to do what they must. And remember that you're talking to the audience, not to yourself. • Characters, you give the story life! Remember to be your character even when you're not speaking, and be sure to react to the other characters.
Performing	• If the audience laughs, stop speaking until they can hear you again. • If someone talks in the audience, don't pay attention. • If someone walks into the room, don't look at them. • If you make a mistake, pretend it was right. • If a reader forgets to read his or her part, don't signal to the reader, just skip over it or make something up.

Booker T. Washington

CONNECTIONS

Literature Connection—*More Than Anything Else* by Marie Bradby

More Than Anything Else is a fictionalized but historically accurate snapshot into the boyhood life of Booker T. Washington. The theme throughout is Washington's desire to learn to read "more than anything else," and the book concludes as Washington begins to understand printed words.

Content Connections—Black History, Biographies, and Social Studies

Booker T. Washington takes the reader beyond Washington's childhood and into his many accomplishments as an adult. This script is especially appropriate for units of study during Black History month.

OBJECTIVE

Students will summarize and paraphrase information in texts (e.g., includes the main idea and significant supporting details of a reading selection).

VOCABULARY

1. Introduce the key vocabulary words from the script. Write each word on the board.

2. Describe the meaning of each word and point out its use in the script.

3. Work together as a class to create a word web for each vocabulary word. Write the first vocabulary word in the center of a sheet of chart paper. Put a circle around the word. Then guide students in brainstorming related words, phrases, and examples to add to the web. Write students' responses around the vocabulary word and connect each one to the center circle in order to create a web. Post the word webs around the room for students' reference.

- **ignorance**—not having knowledge

- **plantation**—a large farm

- **prosper**—to do well

- **success**—an accomplishment that is done well

- **trade**—a job requiring a skill

BEFORE THE READER'S THEATER

1. Read the title of the script and discuss the various roles. Then ask students to make predictions about the selection. What do they think this reader's theater will be about? Is it fiction or nonfiction? Why do they think so? Does anyone know anything about a man named Booker T. Washington?

2. Introduce the Summary Pyramid graphic organizer (page 16 or summarypyramid.pdf). Demonstrate its use by reading the first two lines of the script and picking out the important words for the graphic organizer. Tell the class that they will finish the graphic organizer after reading the script.

Booker T. Washington (cont.)

BEFORE THE READER'S THEATER (cont.)

3. Read the script aloud, modeling appropriate reading strategies while you read. To help build fluency and comprehension, it is important for students to hear the script read aloud before practicing on their own.

DURING THE READER'S THEATER

1. Divide the class into groups of five to read and practice the script. As they read, they are to look for the main idea of the script.

2. Students need to decide which character they will play and then highlight their parts in the script (Readers 1–5). They should also mark with a star any places where they need to pause while reading.

3. Give students a few minutes to practice reading with expression in their voices. Additionally, students may decide on a few props or materials to use during their reading. They need to use materials that can be easily acquired or assembled in the classroom.

4. After they have finished practicing, have each group perform the reader's theater for the rest of the class. You may also want them to perform for another class.

AFTER THE READER'S THEATER

1. As a class, finish filling in key words on the Summary Pyramid graphic organizer.

2. Have students conduct an Internet search for more information about Booker T. Washington.

3. Have students write an informative letter to a student in another class telling them at least three new facts they learned about Booker T. Washington.

RESPONSE QUESTIONS

Group Discussion Questions

- Who is the speaker on the "All" parts of the script?
- What is the theme or lesson taught by this reading selection? (Suggested answers: Work for your goal; Education improves lives; One person can make a difference.)
- Why does the monument compare ignorance to a veil?

Written Response Question

- What sort of person do you think Booker T. Washington was? Why do you think so?

Name_____ Date _____

Summary Pyramid

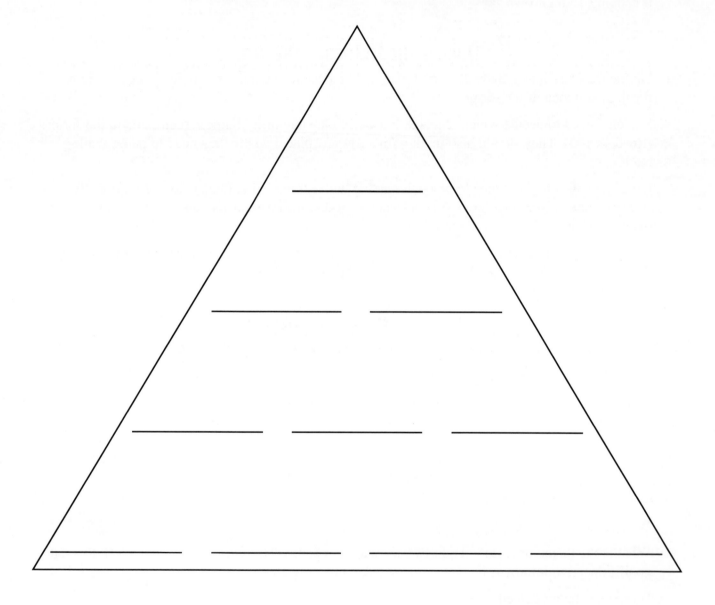

Booker T. Washington

BY CATHY DAVIS

A reader's theater with five parts

Reader 1: Booker T. Washington was born in 1856 on a plantation in Virginia.

Reader 5: His mother was a slave, and he went to work when he was a young boy.

Reader 3: It was illegal for a slave to learn to read and write, so Booker didn't get to go to school.

Reader 1: After the Civil War, the slaves were freed, but many of them couldn't find work.

Reader 2: Booker's stepfather was lucky to get a job packing salt in West Virginia. So, the rest of the family followed him there.

Reader 4: Booker was only nine years old, but he went to work in the salt mines.

All: I want to learn. It's not my fault.
But the days are long packing salt.

Reader 5: Booker wanted an education and used his free time to go to school whenever he could. But, he didn't get to go very often.

Reader 1: When he was 16, he left home to go to a new school for African Americans called the Hampton Institute.

Booker T. Washington *(cont.)*

Reader 4: Booker didn't know if the school would let him in.

Reader 5: General Samuel Armstrong ran the Hampton Institute.

All: I've heard about your new school.
I'm hungry and broke, but I'm not a fool.

Reader 2: General Armstrong was impressed with Booker.

Reader 4: Armstrong found a friend to pay the school fees.

Reader 3: He also gave Booker a job as the school janitor.

Reader 1: Booker spent three years studying at Hampton. Then he taught at a school for African American children.

Reader 3: In 1879, he came back to Hampton as an instructor.

Reader 2: He was put in charge of a program for 75 American Indians.

Reader 4: Booker's work with these students was such a success that Booker was given the chance to head a new school for African American students in Tuskegee, Alabama.

Reader 5: Under Booker's leadership, the Tuskegee Institute became one of the best African American schools in the country.

Reader 2: The students at Tuskegee learned the skills needed to get better paying jobs.

Booker T. Washington *(cont.)*

All: I want each student to have a trade.
That's what I want to foster.
Education is the key to help my people prosper.

Reader 4:   Booker wrote books and became a well-known public speaker.

Reader 1:   He was the first African American person to be invited to have dinner in the White House.

Reader 5:   Booker died in 1915.

Reader 3:   Years later, the Tuskegee Institute became Tuskegee University, a college well-known for its science, engineering, and veterinary medicine programs.

All: I started the school in a run down shack.
And my, oh my, how it's grown.
Look at the different college degrees
All from the seeds I have sown.

Reader 2:   The Booker T. Washington Monument stands today at the center of Tuskegee University.

Reader 1:   These words are written on it about Booker:

Reader 4:   "He lifted the veil of ignorance from his people."

Reader 5:   Booker T. Washington is remembered as one of the most important African American educators of his time.

The Rhyming Author

CONNECTIONS

Literature Connection—*What Do Authors Do?* by Eileen Christelow

What Do Authors Do? uses a whimsical comic-strip format to show the steps that a real author goes through, from generating an idea all the way to publication.

Content Connections—Authors and Biographies

The Rhyming Author covers the life of Dr. Seuss, an author familiar to third grade students. It is a great addition to a lesson about the writing process.

OBJECTIVE

Students will use prior knowledge and experience to understand and respond to new information.

VOCABULARY

1. Introduce the key vocabulary words from the script. Write each word on the board.

2. Describe the meaning of each word and point out its use in the script.

3. Work with students to develop their oral language. Create a sentence frame for each vocabulary word. Write the sentence frames on the board. For example, The illustrator drew _____ for the _____. Then ask students to complete the sentence in another way.

   - **illustrator**—a person who draws pictures for a book
   - **primer**—a small book for teaching children to read
   - **professor**—a teacher at a college or university
   - **rejected**—turned down
   - **rhymes**—words with the same ending sounds
   - **screenplay**—the written form of a story prepared for a movie

BEFORE THE READER'S THEATER

1. Read the title of the script and discuss the various roles. Then ask students to make predictions about the selection. What do they think this script will be about? Is it fiction or nonfiction? Why do they think so? What is an author?

2. Read aloud the first five lines and ask the following questions: What do you know about Dr. Seuss or his books? Which of his books have you read?

The Rhyming Author *(cont.)*

BEFORE THE READER'S THEATER *(cont.)*

3. Introduce the K-W-L Chart graphic organizer (page 22 or kwlchart.pdf). Tell students that this graphic organizer will help to categorize information about what they know, what they want to know, and later, what they learned about the topic. Lead the class in completing the first two columns of the K-W-L Chart. Tell the class that they will finish the graphic organizer after the reading.

4. Read the script aloud, modeling appropriate reading strategies while you read. To help build fluency and comprehension, it is important for students to hear the script read aloud before practicing on their own.

DURING THE READER'S THEATER

1. Divide the class into groups of seven to read and practice the script.

2. Students need to decide which character they will play and then highlight their parts in the script (Readers 1–7). They should also mark with a star any places where they need to pause while reading.

3. Give students a few minutes to practice reading with expression in their voices. Additionally, students may decide on a few props or materials to use during their reading. They need to use materials that can be easily acquired or assembled in the classroom.

4. After they have finished practicing, have each group perform the reader's theater for the rest of the class. You may also want them to perform for another class.

AFTER THE READER'S THEATER

1. As a class, fill in the "What I Learned" column of the K-W-L Chart graphic organizer.

2. Read other stories about Dr. Seuss.

3. Encourage students to search for more information about another favorite author.

RESPONSE QUESTIONS

Group Discussion Questions

*   How did Theodor Geisel get the pen name Dr. Seuss?

*   Why do you think Dr. Seuss kept trying to succeed after getting rejected so many times? How might things have been different if he hadn't kept trying?

*   Why do you think Ted's publisher wanted him to use only 250 words in a book for first graders?

*   Why do you think Dr. Seuss wrote *The Cat in the Hat* in rhyme?

Written Response Question

*   If you were just learning to read, would Dr. Seuss books be a good choice? Why?

Name_____ Date _____

K-W-L Chart

K	W	L

The Rhyming Author

BY CATHY DAVIS

A reader's theater with seven parts

Reader 1: This is the story of a famous author and illustrator.

Reader 5: He wrote mostly in rhymes.

Reader 4: His name was Theodor Geisel.

All: Ted for short.

Reader 6: He became known around the world as Dr. Seuss.

Reader 2: You probably have read some of his work,

Reader 3: such as *How the Grinch Stole Christmas*,

Reader 1: *Horton Hears a Who*,

Reader 5: or *Green Eggs and Ham*.

Reader 7: Ted was born on March 2, 1904, in Massachusetts.

Reader 2: When he was a little boy, his mother chanted bedtime rhymes to help him get to sleep.

All: Can, man, pan, ran

Reader 1: He later said that he learned how to make rhymes from his mother.

The Rhyming Author *(cont.)*

Reader 7: Ted's parents knew that he had an active imagination,

Reader 3: because he was always drawing strange things in his notebooks at school.

Reader 4: Ted went to Dartmouth College and Oxford University.

Reader 2: He had plans to become an English professor, but he didn't do that.

Reader 1: Instead, he went to work writing articles and drawing cartoons for magazines.

Reader 3: He created ads for the Standard Oil Company.

Reader 5: Ted did this for many years.

Reader 2: In 1936, he wrote his first book *And to Think I Saw It on Mulberry Street*.

Reader 7: Forty-three publishers rejected it.

Reader 4: But, a friend published it for him, and the book had some success.

Reader 3: Ted had published the book under the pen name "Dr. Seuss."

Reader 6: He used the name Seuss because it was his mother's maiden name.

The Rhyming Author *(cont.)*

Reader 5: He added "Dr." to it because he had planned to be a professor.

Reader 1: Ted was a captain in the army during World War II.

Reader 2: Then the army sent him to Hollywood to write screenplays.

Reader 7: He won Oscars for his films.

Reader 4: Then came the 1950s.

Reader 5: Students at that time learned to read with the Dick and Jane primers.

Reader 6: The same words were repeated over and over in these books.

All: Dick and Jane, Dick and Jane.

Reader 1: In 1954, a man named John Hershey wrote a report about the schools.

Reader 2: He said that one reason the children had trouble learning to read was because the primers were so boring.

All: Dick and Jane, Dick and Jane.
I'm sick of Dick and Jane.

Reader 3: Ted's publisher thought that Ted could write a book that would be fun to read.

The Rhyming Author *(cont.)*

Reader 4: That's when he wrote *The Cat in the Hat*.

Reader 1: It was an instant success.

Reader 7: In 1960, he wrote *Green Eggs and Ham*.

Reader 3: Ted wrote some other books quickly.

Reader 4: Once, he saw a herd of elephants in Africa and then wrote *The Lorax* in 45 minutes.

Reader 7: In 1986, he wrote a book for adults called *2*.

Reader 2: Dr. Seuss died in 1991.

Reader 1: He had written 44 children's books.

Reader 6: His books have been published in 15 languages and have sold millions of copies.

Reader 4: Dr. Seuss's books have been turned into television specials, a Broadway musical, and a motion picture.

Reader 3: Today, school children remember Dr. Seuss by celebrating his birthday each year with the Read Across America program.

Reader 5: Dr. Seuss continues to entertain us and make reading fun.

Black Bart the Po8

CONNECTIONS

Literature Connection—*How I Spent My Summer Vacation* by Mark Teague

How I Spent My Summer Vacation is the story of Wallace, a boy with a wild imagination. Wallace shocks his teacher and classmates with his essay about traveling west and being kidnapped by cowboys.

Content Connections—Biographies, Social Studies, Western Movement

Black Bart the Po8 can be used as an introduction to a lesson about the Western Movement. It tells the tale of a true wild west outlaw and stagecoach robber. Students will learn about an important period of American history as they read about this successful thief.

OBJECTIVE

Students will summarize and paraphrase information in texts (e.g., includes the main idea and significant supporting details of a reading selection).

VOCABULARY

1. Introduce the key vocabulary words from the script. Write each word on the board.

2. Describe the meaning of each word and point out its use in the script.

3. Challenge the class to a game of team charades. Divide the class into small groups. Ask each group to choose a vocabulary word to act out for the class. Give each group three minutes to decide how to demonstrate its assigned word. As each group acts out the word, challenge the others to guess the word.

   - **derby**—a fancy hat

   - **outlaw**—a person in trouble with the law

   - **stagecoach**—a vehicle pulled by horses that can carry passengers and mail

   - **strongbox**—a padlocked, wooden box covered with iron bands

BEFORE THE READER'S THEATER

1. Share a picture or drawing of a stagecoach with students. Point out where both the driver and the passengers ride. Read the title of the script and discuss the various roles.

2. Ask students to make predictions about the time and setting of the script. What do they think the script is about? Is it fiction or nonfiction? Why do they think so? What do they think might be the setting of this script? Has anyone watched a western movie on television?

3. Display the Box Summary graphic organizer (page 29 or boxsummary.pdf). Explain that it is a tool to help them take notes about the important words in the script. Model how to use the graphic organizer by filling in a few key words from the beginning of the script. Tell students that they will complete the rest of the graphic organizer after they have read the script.

Black Bart the Po8 *(cont.)*

BEFORE THE READER'S THEATER *(cont.)*

4. Read the script aloud, modeling appropriate reading strategies while you read. To help build fluency and comprehension, it is important for students to hear the script read aloud before practicing on their own.

DURING THE READER'S THEATER

1. Split the class into groups of six to read and practice the script. As they read, they are to look for the main idea of the script.

2. Students need to decide which character they will play and then highlight their parts in the script (Readers 1–6). They should also mark with a star any places where they need to pause while reading.

3. Give students a few minutes to practice reading with expression in their voices. Additionally, students may decide on a few props or materials to use during their reading. They need to use materials that can be easily acquired or assembled in the classroom.

4. After they have finished practicing, have each group perform the reader's theater for the rest of the class. You may also want them to perform for another class.

AFTER THE READER'S THEATER

1. Bring the class back together and use the script to complete the Box Summary graphic organizer.

2. Read other stories about the wild west. Encourage students to find both fiction and nonfiction books on the topic.

RESPONSE QUESTIONS

Group Discussion Questions

- How did Charles Boles rob his first stagecoach? Why do you think he was able to get away with the robberies for so many years?
- How did Charles Boles get the name "Black Bart the Po8?" What was unusual about him?
- Wells Fargo's motto was "Wells Fargo never forgets." Was it true in this case?

Written Response Question

- Do you think that Charles Boles was a brave man? Why or why not?

Famous People

Graphic Organizer

Name_____ Date _____

Box Summary

Black Bart the Po8

BY CATHY DAVIS

A reader's theater with six parts

Reader 4: This is the story of Black Bart, the Po8!

Reader 2: He was a stagecoach robber who wrote poems.

Reader 5: He was not like any other outlaw.

Reader 3: In the days before airplanes and automobiles, people traveled west to California by stagecoach.

Reader 6: These stagecoaches often carried money for businesses.

Reader 5: This made them a target for thieves.

All: Black Bart the Po8!

Reader 4: Black Bart staged his first robbery on July 26, 1875.

Reader 1: A Wells Fargo stagecoach began to climb a steep mountain pass in northern California.

Reader 2: Unknown to the stagecoach driver, Black Bart was waiting.

Reader 3: The outlaw had already tied several sticks down in the brush up ahead beside the road.

Reader 4: As the stagecoach went by, Black Bart stepped in front of it and pointed a shotgun at the driver.

Black Bart the Po8 *(cont.)*

Reader 6: He wore a flour sack over his head with holes cut for his eyes.

Reader 2: "Please throw down the box!" the outlaw said politely.

Reader 5: And he added in a deep voice: "If he dares to shoot, give him a solid volley, boys!"

Reader 3: The driver looked around and saw what he thought were six rifles aimed at him.

Reader 5: Thinking he was outnumbered, the driver reached under his seat and pulled out the Wells Fargo strongbox.

Reader 6: The box was thrown to the ground beside the masked man.

Reader 3: Black Bart began loading his pockets with the bags of gold coins.

Reader 2: Then he waited for the stagecoach to leave.

Reader 4: The stagecoach driver stopped the stagecoach and walked back down the road to get the empty strongbox.

Reader 1: That's when he discovered that he had been tricked.

Reader 6: The outlaw was gone, but the sticks were still there!

Reader 5: Black Bart's real name was Charles Boles.

Reader 4: No one would ever have guessed he robbed banks.

Black Bart the Po8 *(cont.)*

Reader 2: Boles was over 50 years old, had gray hair, and carried a cane.

Reader 1: He lived in the finest hotels and ate at the finest restaurants.

Reader 6: Boles dressed well, wearing derby hats and diamond rings.

Reader 3: Charles Boles robbed 28 Wells Fargo stagecoaches over the next seven years.

Reader 2: He stole a total of $18,000 from the bank.

Reader 5: He left written poems at his robberies and signed them "Black Bart the Po8."

Reader 1: Oh, now I get it, Po8 means "poet." And so the legend of Black Bart the Po8 was born.

Reader 2: Black Bart never fired his shotgun or hurt anyone during is many holdups.

Reader 4: Passengers remembered his polite manner.

Reader 5: And how he refused to take anything from women travelers.

Reader 3: When Boles was finally captured, he served four years in jail.

Reader 6: No one knows for sure what happened to him when he was released.

Reader 1: He just seemed to disappear!

All: Black Bart the Po8!

The Radio Show that Frightened Thousands

CONNECTIONS

Literature Connection—*Guys from Space* by Daniel Pinkwater

Guys from Space is a humorous science fiction selection complete with aliens and a spaceship ride to a distant planet.

Content Connections—Social Studies, Science Fiction

The Radio Show that Frightened Thousands is the true account of the panic that took place during Orson Welles's 1938 radio broadcast warning of a Martian invasion.

OBJECTIVE

Students will use prior knowledge and experience to understand and respond to new information.

VOCABULARY

1. Introduce the key vocabulary words from the script. Write each word on the board.

2. Describe the meaning of each word and point out its use in the script.

3. Review the definition of each vocabulary word. As you do, ask students to complete your statement by saying the vocabulary word. For example, say to students, "The _____ fell from the sky." Students should respond by saying *meteor*.

   - **astronomer**—a scientist that studies planets and space

   - **broadcast**—sounds or pictures sent out by television or radio

   - **entertainment**—anything done for fun

   - **hoax**—a trick

   - **meteor**—a rock from space

BEFORE THE READER'S THEATER

1. Read the title of the script and discuss the various roles. Then ask students to make predictions about the selection. What do they think the script will be about? Is it fiction or nonfiction? Why do they think so? Does anyone listen to the radio? What kinds of things do they hear on the radio?

The Radio Show that Frightened Thousands *(cont.)*

BEFORE THE READER'S THEATER *(cont.)*

2. Introduce the Question Strips graphic organizer (page 35 or questionstrips.pdf). Give each student a copy of the graphic organizer

3. The question strips contain the following words: *who, what, when, why, how,* and *what if.* After practicing the script, students will work in groups to write one question for each strip.

4. Read the script aloud, modeling appropriate reading strategies while you read. To help build fluency and comprehension, it is important for students to hear the script read aloud before practicing on their own.

DURING THE READER'S THEATER

1. Divide the class into groups of six to read and practice the script.

2. Students need to decide which character they will play and then highlight their parts in the script (Readers 1–6). They should also mark with a star any places where they need to pause while reading.

3. Give students a few minutes to practice reading with expression in their voices. Additionally, students may decide on a few props or materials to use during their reading. They need to use materials that can be easily acquired or assembled in the classroom.

4. After they have finished practicing, have each group perform the reader's theater for the rest of the class. You may also want them to perform for another class.

AFTER THE READER'S THEATER

1. After reading the script, have the groups work together to finish the Question Strips graphic organizer. Then bring the class back together and have the groups share the completed questions and discuss possible answers.

2. Have students find other science fiction books that they would be interested in reading.

RESPONSE QUESTIONS

Group Discussion Questions

- What kinds of things do you think people did for entertainment before television?

- What does your family do if the electricity is out or if the TV isn't working?

Written Response Question

- Would you have been scared if you had heard the "War of the Worlds" radio program? Why or why not?

Name_____ Date _____

Question Strips

Who?	

What?	

When?	

Why?	

How?	

What If?	

The Radio Show that Frightened Thousands

BY CATHY DAVIS

A reader's theater with six parts

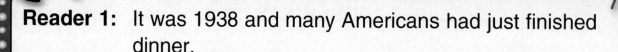

Reader 1: It was 1938 and many Americans had just finished dinner.

Reader 6: Television didn't exist, but families had other kinds of entertainment.

Reader 2: It was the Golden Age of Broadcasting, a time when the whole family gathered around the radio after dinner.

Reader 4: Everyone had a favorite radio program because there were shows for all ages.

Reader 5: On October 30, 1938, six million listeners were enjoying orchestra music on the radio.

Reader 1: Then suddenly, the music stopped and a reporter delivered an important message.

Reader 4: Astronomers had seen blue flames shooting up from planet Mars.

Reader 3: Everyone wondered what that could mean, but the radio broadcast returned to the regular music program.

Reader 6: Once again the music was interrupted for a special news bulletin.

Reader 5: A meteor had fallen to Earth and landed on a farm near Grover's Mill, New Jersey.

Reader 6: More announcements came throughout the night.

The Radio Show that Frightened Thousands *(cont.)*

Reader 2: Families in New Jersey were glued to their radio sets.

Reader 1: Martians had landed on Earth and were blasting the crowd around them with deadly heat-rays.

Reader 4: The army was called in, but the Martians won the battle.

Reader 5: They began marching and releasing a poisonous black gas.

Reader 2: Many radio listeners panicked. Hundreds called the police.

Reader 4: Some people hid in their cellars, while others got into their cars and drove away.

Reader 5: Before the night was over, the people learned that the program was a hoax.

Reader 2: An actor named Orson Welles had done the program as an early Halloween spook story.

Reader 6: He had made an announcement before the show that the people were about to hear a radio play called "War of the Worlds."

Reader 1: However, many listeners had tuned in late and missed that announcement. They thought it was really happening.

Reader 4: In the 1950s, television overtook the Golden Age of Broadcasting.

Reader 5: But Orson Welles proved how believable the radio could be.

The Dust Bowl

CONNECTIONS

Literature Connection—*Leah's Pony* by Elizabeth Friedrich

Leah's Pony is realistic historical fiction about the hardship of life on a family farm during the drought of the 1930s. Personal sacrifice and helping one another are the main themes, as Leah's neighbors pitch in and prevent her family from losing everything at a public auction.

Content Connection—Social Studies

The Dust Bowl relates, through the eyes of farm children, to a bleak time in American history known as the Dust Bowl. This script builds background for a better understanding of *Leah's Pony*.

OBJECTIVE

Students will use text organizers (e.g., headings, topic and summary sentences, graphic features, typeface, chapter titles) to determine the main ideas and to locate information in a text.

VOCABULARY

1. Introduce the key vocabulary words from the script. Write each word on the board.

2. Describe the meaning of each word and point out its use in the script.

3. Play an example game with students. Read the first vocabulary word. Then state both an example and a nonexample of the word, and ask students to discriminate between them. For example, say to students, "If anything I say is an example of drought, say 'drought.' If not, don't say anything." Provide choices such as *no rain* (example) and *flooding* (nonexample).

   - **churned**—stirred using a round and round motion
   - **drought**—a long period without rain
   - **thistles**—prickly plants
   - **topsoil**—the top layer of the soil where plants grow
   - **wedged**—pushed into a tight place

The Dust Bowl (cont.)

BEFORE THE READER'S THEATER

1. Read the title of the script and discuss the various roles. Then ask students to make predictions about the selection. What do they think this reader's theater will be about? Is it fiction or nonfiction? Why do they think so? What do they think a dust bowl is?

2. Lead a discussion about natural disasters such as floods, tornadoes, storms, snow blizzards, and earthquakes and how we deal with each one. Ask students to share any information they know about this topic.

3. Read the script aloud, modeling appropriate reading strategies while you read. To help build fluency and comprehension, it is important for students to hear the script read aloud before practicing on their own.

DURING THE READER'S THEATER

1. Divide the class into groups of seven to read and practice the script. As they read, they are to look for details of ways the families dealt with the dust storms.

2. Students need to decide which character they will play and then highlight their parts in the script (Readers 1–6 and Narrator). They should also mark with a star any places where they need to pause while reading.

3. Give students a few minutes to practice reading with expression in their voices. Additionally, students may decide on a few props or materials to use during their reading. They need to use materials that can be easily acquired or assembled in the classroom.

4. After they have finished practicing, have each group perform the reader's theater for the rest of the class. You may also want them to perform for another class.

AFTER THE READER'S THEATER

1. Bring the class back together. Display the Main Idea and Details graphic organizer (page 40 or mainideaanddetails.pdf). Write the following statement at the top: The families tried many ways to fight the dust. Help students brainstorm and look through the script to find details to support the statement.

2. Have students conduct an Internet search for more information about farming.

RESPONSE QUESTIONS

Group Discussion Questions

- What caused the dust bowl? Was it started on purpose?

- What caused it to end? Could it happen again?

Written Response Question

- How would you have felt if you had been there on Black Sunday?

Name_____ Date _____

Main Idea and Details

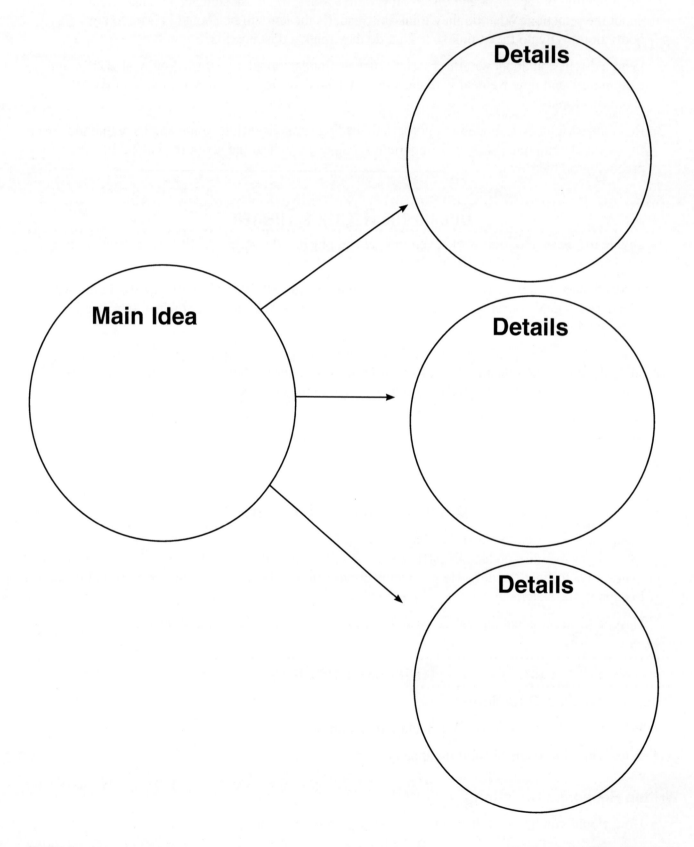

The Dust Bowl

BY CATHY DAVIS

A reader's theater with seven parts

Narrator: This is the story of the dust bowl, a terrible time in American history.

Reader 1: It was a time when Mother Nature went wild!

Narrator: It happened during the Great Depression.

Reader 5: We lived through it.

All: We are the children of the dust bowl, and this is our story.

Reader 4: Our parents were settlers who came to the Midwest and Southern Plains.

Reader 2: They had been farmers in the East and planned to farm the new land.

Reader 6: They brought with them the farming techniques used in the East.

Narrator: But the new land was different. It was a flat, treeless place where the wind blew all the time.

Reader 3: It might rain, and it might not.

All: Dust in my ears, dust in my eyes.
Dust, dust, makes Mama cry.

The Dust Bowl *(cont.)*

Narrator: The farmers cut the ground with steel plows in order to plant wheat because the price of wheat was high.

Reader 5: Papa said, "The rain will follow the plow," and for a while, it did.

Narrator: But in 1931, an eight-year drought began.

Reader 2: Without rain, the crops dried up, and the fields just blew away.

Reader 1: One hot, dry summer followed another.

Reader 5: The winds became stronger and gathered the dust up into huge black clouds.

Reader 4: The dust churned in the sky and blocked out the sun.

Reader 6: These storms turned day into night.

Narrator: The worst dust storm happened on April 14, 1935. This day was called Black Sunday.

Reader 1: A dark cloud appeared, traveling faster than a truck.

Reader 4: The crows tried to fly ahead of it, but they weren't fast enough.

Reader 5: And, all the while, it kept getting darker and darker.

The Dust Bowl *(cont.)*

Reader 6:　We thought it was the end of the world!

Reader 2:　Everything Papa had worked for was destroyed.

Reader 3:　Many of our neighbors gave up and moved away.

Narrator:　But most farmers stayed. They wouldn't give up.

Reader 1:　When we had no grain to feed our animals, we fed them thistles.

Reader 5:　When the thistles dried up, we chopped up weeds for them to eat.

Reader 3:　Somehow, we hung on.

All:　Dust in my bed, dust in the wind.
Dust, dust, dust without an end.

Reader 6:　We fought the dust in every way we could.

Narrator:　We put sheets over windows and hung blankets over the doors.

Reader 4:　We wedged cloth in every crack of the house.

Reader 2:　We tried to keep it out, but it found a way in.

Reader 3:　Inside our farmhouse, it was hot and dusty. It was hard for me to breathe.

The Dust Bowl *(cont.)*

Reader 1: We tied handkerchiefs over our mouths and noses.

Reader 5: We made tents of wet sheets and put them over our beds, but still we coughed up dust.

Narrator: In 1935, the federal government got involved. Thirty-five million acres of crops had been destroyed, and 100 million acres had lost all or most of their topsoil.

Reader 1: More than 75% of the United States had been affected.

Reader 2: The government started the Soil Conservation Service to help the farmers.

Reader 3: They showed us new ways to farm, and they paid us a dollar an acre to try them out.

Reader 5: We learned to plant some areas with grass and to plant lines of trees to break the wind.

Reader 6: We learned to plow in strips instead of plowing a whole field.

Reader 4: We didn't plant wheat year after year. We learned to rotate the crops to enrich the soil.

Narrator: At last, the rains came in 1939 and ended the long drought. The time of the dust bowl was over.

All: Dust on my pillow, dust in my shoes.
Dust, dust, we paid our dues.

The Story of Basketball

CONNECTIONS

Literature Connection—*Allie's Basketball Dream* by Barbara E. Barber

Allie's Basketball Dream is a delightful fictional story about Allie, a girl who gets a new basketball. Allie learns that hard work and practice pay off as she gains confidence in herself while improving her basketball skills.

Content Connections—Social Studies, Physical Education

The Story of Basketball covers the true events of how a YMCA instructor invented the game of basketball using half-bushel peach baskets and a soccer ball. This reader's theater would be a great way to introduce a lesson on the history of other sports.

OBJECTIVE

Students will understand structural patterns or organization in informational texts (e.g., chronological, logical, or sequential order; compare-and-contrast; cause-and-effect; proposition and support).

VOCABULARY

1. Introduce the key vocabulary words from the script. Write each word on the board.

2. Describe the meaning of each word and point out its use in the script.

3. Help students make word associations for the selected vocabulary words. Ask them questions about linking other words with one of the vocabulary words. For example, a word association question for *invent* might be, "Which world goes with *create*?"

   - **bushel**—a unit of measurement

   - **deadline**—the date when something is due

   - **instructor**—a teacher

   - **invent**—to make something new

   - **janitor**—a person who cleans

   - **rowdy**—loud and out of control

BEFORE THE READER'S THEATER

1. Read the title of the script and discuss the various roles. Then ask students to make predictions about the selection. What do they think this reader's theater will be about? Is it fiction or nonfiction? Why do they think so?

2. Write the word *basketball* in the middle of a web organizer on the board. Ask the class what they already know about basketball. Fill in the rest of the web with key words and phrases given by the students about basketball.

The Story of Basketball (cont.)

3. Tell the class that the script explains how the game of basketball was created. Explain that the events occur in a certain sequence or order. Display the Story Map graphic organizer (page 47 or storymap.pdf) and tell the class that they will complete the map together after reading the script.

4. Read the script aloud, modeling appropriate reading strategies while you read. To help build fluency and comprehension, it is important for students to hear the script read aloud before practicing on their own.

DURING THE READER'S THEATER

1. Divide the class into groups of five to read and practice the script.

2. Students need to decide which character they will play and then highlight their parts in the script (Readers 1–5). They should also mark with a star any places where they need to pause while reading.

3. Give students a few minutes to practice reading with expression in their voices. Additionally, students may decide on a few props or materials to use during their reading. They need to use materials that can be easily acquired or assembled in the classroom.

4. After they have finished practicing, have each group perform the reader's theater for the rest of the class. You may also want them to perform for another class.

AFTER THE READER'S THEATER

1. As a class, complete the Story Map graphic organizer.

2. Have students choose another sport and research its history.

RESPONSE QUESTIONS

Group Discussion Questions

- What did you learn that you didn't already know about basketball?

- Why do you think that the one class was so hard for the PE teachers to handle during the winter? Why do you think that outdoor games wouldn't work inside the gym?

- James Naismith believed that he could help others through sports. What kinds of things can be learned from playing sports, besides the game's rules?

- How do you think that James and his students got the balls out of the baskets when a shot was made?

Written Response Question

- What kinds of activities do you do indoors during PE class? Would you like indoor PE if you only did drills and exercises? Why or why not?

Name_____ Date _____

Story Map

Title:

_____

Setting:

_____

_____

_____

Characters:

_____

_____

Problem:

_____

_____

_____

Events:

_____

_____

_____

Solution:

_____

_____

The Story of Basketball

BY CATHY DAVIS

A reader's theater with five parts

All: Bounce, bounce, dribble, pass
Shoot that basket. Dunk it fast.

Reader 1: That's the sound of basketball, a game played by more than 300 million people.

Reader 4: This is the story of how the game came to be.

Reader 3: A Canadian man named James Naismith was studying to be a minister.

Reader 2: He had always been a good athlete.

Reader 5: He worked as a physical-education instructor to help pay for his education.

Reader 4: James believed that he could minister through athletics.

Reader 1: His teachers thought sports were a waste of his time.

Reader 3: In 1890, James enrolled at the YMCA International Training School in Springfield, Massachusetts.

Reader 2: The students enjoyed outdoor sports like track and football, but indoor physical education wasn't much fun—

Reader 1: unless you liked exercises and drills.

The Story of Basketball *(cont.)*

All: We love the fall months. Football's the reason.
But it's a long wait 'til spring baseball season.

Reader 1: Dr. Gulick, head of the PE Department, saw the need for an indoor game to be played during the cold winter months.

Reader 5: One class of men was so sick of the indoor drills that two different instructors asked Dr. Gulick to excuse them from teaching that class.

Reader 3: Dr. Gulick turned the PE class over to James and gave him the assignment of inventing some indoor games for the winter season.

Reader 2: James had only 14 days to come up with a game for his class.

Reader 4: It had to be fair, but not too rough.

Reader 5: At first James thought of bringing outdoor games inside, but that wouldn't work.

Reader 1: He was close to the deadline and at his wit's end.

All: I'm out of ideas, and I'll get the blame.
I can't think of how to create a new game.

Reader 3: Then James remembered a game called "Duck on a Rock."

The Story of Basketball *(cont.)*

Reader 5: Young James and his friends would line up and take turns throwing smaller stones at the big one.

Reader 1: A guard stood off to the side.

Reader 4: If a boy missed hitting the big rock, he had to run and get his stone before the guard tagged him.

Reader 3: This gave James the idea for a new indoor game using a soccer ball.

Reader 1: He wrote 13 rules and called the game "Basket Ball."

Reader 4: James had 18 men in his class.

Reader 3: So, he divided them into two teams of nine each.

Reader 2: He sent the school janitor to find two boxes to use as goals.

Reader 1: He wanted to tie them to the balcony railing up high in the gym.

Reader 5: But, the janitor couldn't find two boxes.

All: Mr. Naismith, I've searched for a box for your crew. But these half-bushel peach baskets will just have to do.

Reader 3: The men tied the baskets to the railing and played the first game of Basket Ball on December 21, 1891.

The Story of Basketball *(cont.)*

Reader 2: It was not an immediate success.

All: This sport is strange. We don't like it at all.
No one can play with a basket and ball.

Reader 4: But the students changed their minds before they went home for Christmas break.

All: We hated the game. We wanted to quit.
But now we think the game is a hit!

Reader 1: Eventually, the game became officially known as basketball.

Reader 5: James Naismith died in 1939, but he had lived to see basketball added to the 1936 Olympics.

All: I didn't get rich, and I didn't have fame.
But I am the man who invented the game.

Reader 3: Today basketball is played in over 20 countries

Reader 2: by men and women, boys and girls

Reader 4: of all ages.

Reader 5: It's played by professionals and on school playgrounds.

All: Whenever you shoot for the hoop and fall short,
Remember how James invented the sport.

The Mountain Lion

CONNECTIONS

Literature Connections—*Brave as a Mountain Lion* by Ann Herbert Scott

Brave as a Mountain Lion is a fictional work about an American Indian boy named Spider. Spider overcomes his fear of being on stage for the school spelling bee by being "brave as a mountain lion."

Content Connections—Animals, Science

The Mountain Lion gives children factual information about this large, wide-ranging feline. Students will learn about the mountain lion's place in the animal kingdom.

OBJECTIVE

Students will use text organizers (e.g., headings, topic and summary sentences, graphic features, typeface, chapter titles) to determine the main ideas and to locate information in a text.

VOCABULARY

1. Introduce the key vocabulary words from the script. Write each word on the board.

2. Describe the meaning of each word and point out its use in the script.

3. Help students make visual connections for the vocabulary words. Organize students into small groups. Give each group a sheet of chart paper and markers. Have each group create a poster with several images that depict the meaning of one of the vocabulary words. Then have each group share its poster with the class.

   - **extraordinary**—unusual; greater than average

   - **crouched**—close to the ground

   - **litter**—animals born to a mother at the same time

   - **prey**—an animal taken by another for food

   - **stalks**—searches for prey

BEFORE THE READER'S THEATER

1. Read the title of the script and discuss the various roles. Then ask students to make predictions about the selection. What do they think this reader's theater will be about? Is it fiction or nonfiction? Why do they think so? Has anyone seen a mountain lion at the zoo? What do they know about this animal?

The Mountain Lion *(cont.)*

BEFORE THE READER'S THEATER *(cont.)*

2. Display the Information Web graphic organizer (page 54 or informationweb.pdf). Read the first 10 lines of the script and lead the class in completing part of the web. So far, what are the big ideas and details in the script? Have students copy the web, leaving room to add details as they read. Suggested headings for Information Web: *Mountain Lion* in center, and *Hunting, Description,* and *Habitat* for the three boxes around the center circle.

3. Read the script aloud, modeling appropriate reading strategies while you read. To help build fluency and comprehension, it is important for students to hear the script read aloud before practicing on their own.

DURING THE READER'S THEATER

1. Divide the class into groups of five to read and practice the script.

2. Students need to decide which character they will play and then highlight their parts in the script (Readers 1–5). They should also mark with a star any places where they need to pause while reading.

3. Give students a few minutes to practice reading with expression in their voices. Additionally, students may decide on a few props or materials to use during their reading. They need to use materials that can be easily acquired or assembled in the classroom.

4. After they have finished practicing, have each group perform the reader's theater for the rest of the class. You may also want them to perform for another class.

AFTER THE READER'S THEATER

1. Give students time to add two details to each heading of their Information Web graphic organizer. Then ask volunteers to share their webs with the class.

2. Read other stories about mountain lions. Encourage students to find both fiction and nonfiction books on the topic.

RESPONSE QUESTIONS

Group Discussion Questions

- In what way does the mountain lion act like a house cat?

- How do you think the mountain lion got some of its names?

- How do you think the ranchers out west feel about the mountain lion? Why do you think so?

- Do you think a mountain lion would attack a human? Why do you think so?

Written Response Question

- Which name for the mountain lion do you like best and why?

Name_____ Date _____

Information Web

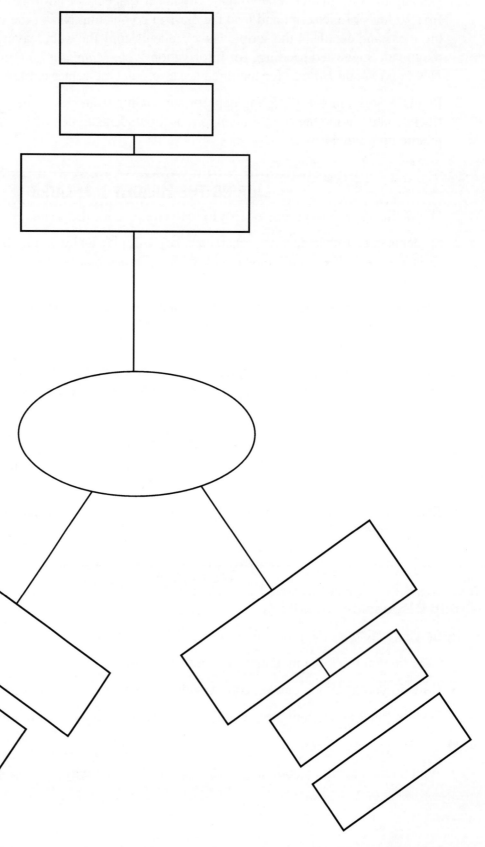

The Mountain Lion

BY CATHY DAVIS

A reader's theater with five parts

Reader 2: This reader's theater is about a big cat.

Reader 3: It's the second largest member of the cat family in North and South America.

Reader 4: We're talking about the mountain lion.

Reader 1: How big is it?

Reader 5: Adult males measure 8 feet long from tail to nose,

Reader 4: and can weigh up to 220 pounds.

Reader 3: The mountain lion is known by many different names.

All: Cougar, puma, mountain lion…

Reader 1: Where does it live?

Reader 2: In the United States, it lives mostly in the West.

Reader 3: But it can also be found in Florida, New England, and around the Appalachian Mountains.

Reader 5: It can live in deserts or forests.

The Mountain Lion *(cont.)*

Reader 1: What do mountain lions eat?

Reader 4: They eat deer, elk, moose, bighorn sheep, and antelope.

Reader 1: You mean its food depends upon where it lives?

Reader 5: Yes, in some areas smaller animals are part of its diet, such as hares, porcupines, and rodents.

Reader 4: Mountain lions also kill and eat cattle, pigs, and horses.

All: Mountain hunter, deer tiger, mountain lion…

Reader 1: How does it hunt?

Reader 3: The mountain lion hunts mostly at night.

Reader 5: It acts much like a house cat while hunting.

Reader 2: It hides and stalks its prey.

Reader 4: Then it jumps from its hiding place in a crouched position.

Reader 1: Can't the prey get away?

Reader 2: Not easily. The mountain lion's powerful rear leg muscles give it extraordinary jumping ability.

Reader 3: It can jump up to 45 feet, so it only takes two or three big leaps to bring the prey down.

The Mountain Lion *(cont.)*

Reader 1: What does a mountain lion look like?

Reader 4: The color of its coat varies according to its region.

Reader 2: It may be a gray, red, or yellowish in color.

Reader 5: Its throat and belly are white.

Reader 3: But the tip of its tail and the backs of its ears are black.

Reader 1: What about the babies?

Reader 2: The mountain lion mother has one to five cubs in a litter, but three is the average number.

Reader 4: The cubs are born blind and are covered with dark spots that disappear as they get older.

Reader 3: The mother keeps the cubs with her for about two years while she teaches them how to hunt.

Reader 1: I've heard that the mountain lion makes an unusual sound.

Reader 2: The mountain lion's cry is frightening.

Reader 5: It sounds like a person screaming in pain.

All: Mountain screamer, sneak cat, mountain lion…

Reader 1: I've learned a lot about the mountain lion.

Learn About Ducks

CONNECTIONS

Literature Connection—*Chibi: A True Story from Japan* by Barbara Brenner and Julia Takaya

Chibi: A True Story from Japan is the story of a mother duck that raises her ducklings in downtown Tokyo. The whole city becomes caught up in the duckling saga, and Chibi, the smallest duckling, is the favorite of the Japanese media.

Content Connections—Animals, Science

Learn About Ducks helps students understand important facts about ducks and teaches them about the diversity of life in the animal world.

OBJECTIVE

Students will summarize and paraphrase information in texts (e.g., includes the main idea and significant supporting details of a reading selection).

VOCABULARY

1. Introduce the key vocabulary words from the script. Write each word on the board.

2. Describe the meaning of each word and point out its use in the script.

3. Have students work in small groups to create posters for the vocabulary words. Fold sheets of chart paper into fourths. Put students into groups and give each group a sheet of the chart paper. Have students use each of the four sections of chart paper to draw a picture that represents the word, write the vocabulary word, the definition, and a sentence that includes the word. Hang the posters around the room for students' reference.

   - **bill**—part of a duck's face

   - **drake**—a male duck

   - **ducklings**—baby ducks

   - **waterproof**—the inability of an object or material to absorb water

   - **waddle**—a way of walking with feet stuck out to the side

BEFORE THE READER'S THEATER

1. Read the title of the script and discuss the various roles. Then ask students to make predictions about the selection. What do they think this script will be about? Is it fiction or nonfiction? Why do they think so? Does this selection remind them of anything else they have read?

2. Read the script aloud, modeling appropriate reading strategies while you read. To help build fluency and comprehension, it is important for students to hear the script read aloud before practicing on their own.

Learn About Ducks *(cont.)*

DURING THE READER'S THEATER

1. Divide the class into groups of five to read and practice the script.

2. Students need to decide which character they will play and then highlight their parts in the script (Ducks 1–4 and Narrator). They should also mark with a star any places where they need to pause while reading.

3. Give students a few minutes to practice reading with expression in their voices. Additionally, students may decide on a few props or materials to use during their reading. They need to use materials that can be easily acquired or assembled in the classroom.

4. After they have finished practicing, have each group perform the reader's theater for the rest of the class. You may also want them to perform for another class.

AFTER THE READER'S THEATER

1. As a class, discuss where the vocabulary words were found. Lead the class in making a Main Idea and Details Web using the graphic organizer (page 60 or mainideaweb.pdf). Students should copy the web outline, read the script, and give suggestions for items to be placed in the middle. The web should contain the following information: *Ducks* in the middle with four branches containing the words *Females, Males, Ducklings,* and *Physical Features*.

2. Have students write a letter to a family member detailing what they have learned about ducks.

RESPONSE QUESTIONS

Group Discussion Questions

- Why is the drake brightly colored but the female ducks are not?
- How do ducks survive the cold winter weather?
- Why are ducks great swimmers but poor walkers?
- Why do you think that ducklings have so many predators?

Written Response Questions

- Would you like to have a duck for a pet? Why or why not?

Main Idea and Details Web

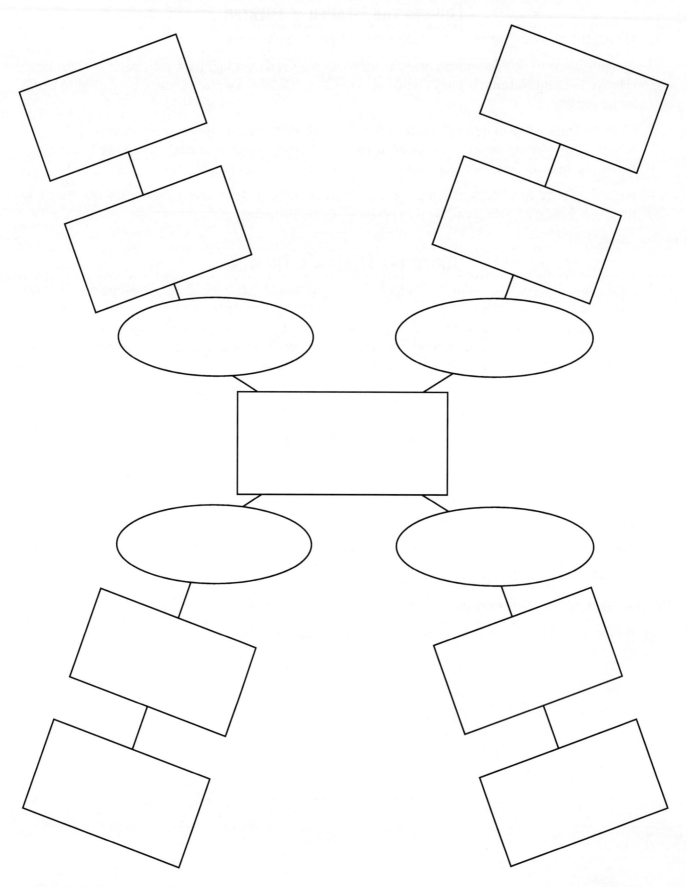

Learn About Ducks

BY CATHY DAVIS

A reader's theater with five parts

Narrator: Ducks are birds with waterproof feathers and webbed feet.

Duck 1: My webbed feet act as paddles for swimming and diving.

Duck 3: Ever tried swimming with flippers on your feet?

Duck 2: It's so much easier!

All: Quack, quack!

Duck 4: We're graceful in the water but waddle clumsily on land.

Duck 2: That's because our legs are set to the sides and toward the rear of our bodies.

Duck 1: Just try walking with your feet to the side!

All: Quack, quack!

Narrator: Ducks live throughout the world in wetlands.

Duck 3: My home might be a marsh, or it could be near a pond, lake, or river.

Duck 1: Some of us even live close to the ocean.

All: Quack, quack!

Learn About Ducks *(cont.)*

Narrator: Most wild ducks weigh between two and four pounds.

Duck 2: That's the weight of one or two of your schoolbooks.

Narrator: Ducks protect themselves from cold water by waterproofing their feathers.

Duck 3: That means we use our bills to rub our feathers with a waxy oil from a gland at the base of our tail.

Duck 4: An instant raincoat!

Duck 2: You should be so lucky!

All: Quack, quack!

Narrator: Under the waxy feathers is a layer of soft fluffy feathers called down.

Duck 1: Down helps keep us warm because it traps air under the outside feathers.

Duck 2: Down comes in handy when the water is freezing.

Duck 4: Ever wonder why a down comforter is so warm?

Duck 1: Now you know the reason why!

All: Quack, quack!

Learn About Ducks *(cont.)*

Duck 1: The males are called drakes.

Narrator: Most drakes have bright-colored feathers to attract a mate.

Duck 3: He is handsome! Oh, so handsome!

All: Quack, quack!

Narrator: The females are called ducks.

Duck 3: That's me, in case you haven't guessed already.

All: Quack, quack!

Duck 3: The brown color helps me blend into my surroundings while sitting on my eggs or taking care of my ducklings.

Narrator: The duck's coloring is a necessary protection against predators.

Duck 3: I need all the help I can get!

Duck 4: The female duck lays between five and twelve eggs.

Duck 3: That is hard work!

Duck 1: The ducklings hatch about a month later.

Duck 3: That's a lot of sitting for me!

Learn About Ducks *(cont.)*

Narrator: A group of ducklings is called a brood.

All: Quack, quack!

Duck 3: Stay together, little ones!

Narrator: The mother duck must keep her brood together so she can protect it.

Duck 2: Turtles, raccoons, hawks, and large fish all eat ducklings.

Duck 3: I told you not to wander off!

All: Quack, quack!

Narrator: Ducklings grow quickly.

Duck 4: We have most of our feathers in a month.

Duck 3: Sniff, sniff. My babies will soon be ready to leave.

Duck 1: We learn to fly a few weeks after that.

Narrator: I hope that you enjoyed learning about ducks.

All: Quack, quack!

The Mud Puppy

CONNECTIONS

Literature Connection—*Fly Traps! Plants that Bite Back* by Martin Jenkins

Fly Traps! Plants that Bite Back combines a fictional narrative with nonfiction inserts and diagrams about carnivorous plants.

Content Connections—Animals, Science

The Mud Puppy turns from plant to animal study as the class learns about an unusual animal found in many states. This script is a good introduction to animal research.

OBJECTIVE

Students will use text organizers (e.g., headings, topic and summary sentences, graphic features, typeface, chapter titles) to determine the main ideas and to locate information in a text.

VOCABULARY

1. Introduce the key vocabulary words from the script. Write each word on the board.

2. Describe the meaning of each word and point out its use in the script.

3. Work with students to develop their oral language. Create a sentence frame for each vocabulary word. For example, Fish use gills to ____. Write the sentence frames on the board. Show students how to complete the first sentence frame. Then ask them to complete the sentence in another way. Repeat this process with the other sentence frames.

   - **cavity**—a hollowed-out space

   - **gills**—an organ that obtains oxygen from water

   - **hibernate**—to spend the winter in a resting state

   - **predator**—an animal that eats another animal

   - **salamander**—a lizard-like animal

   - **slimy**—covered with slime

BEFORE THE READER'S THEATER

1. Read the title of the script and discuss the various roles. Ask students to make predictions about the selection. What do they think this script will be about? Is it fiction or nonfiction? Why do they think so? What could a mud puppy be?

2. Display the Brainstorm Web graphic organizer (page 67 or brainstormweb.pdf) for students.

3. Read the script aloud, modeling appropriate reading strategies while you read. To help build fluency and comprehension, it is important for students to hear the script read aloud before practicing on their own.

The Mud Puppy *(cont.)*

During the Reader's Theater

1. Divide the class into groups of five to read and practice the script.

2. Students need to decide which character they will play and then highlight their parts in the script (Readers 1–5). They should also mark with a star any places where they need to pause while reading.

3. Give students a few minutes to practice reading with expression in their voices. Additionally, students may decide on a few props or materials to use during their reading. They need to use materials that can be easily acquired or assembled in the classroom.

4. After they have finished practicing, have each group perform the reader's theater for the rest of the class. You may also want them to perform for another class. Students need to decide on their parts and then highlight them. They should also mark any places where they need to pause while reading.

After the Reader's Theater

1. Bring the class together to complete the Brainstorm Web graphic organizer.

2. Have students choose another animal to research. Students should prepare a short presentation for the class to share what they have learned about this animal.

Response Questions

Group Discussion Questions

Show a map of the United States and point out the Great Lakes and areas south of Georgia. Then ask the following questions:

- Does the mud puppy live in our area? When might you have seen one?

- How do you think this animal got the name "mud puppy" and "waterdog"?

- Why should you be careful if you find one?

- How does its coloring help it against predators?

- What other animals do you know about that use color for protection?

Written Response Question

- Would you like a mud puppy for a pet? Why or why not?

Name_____ Date _____

Brainstorm Web

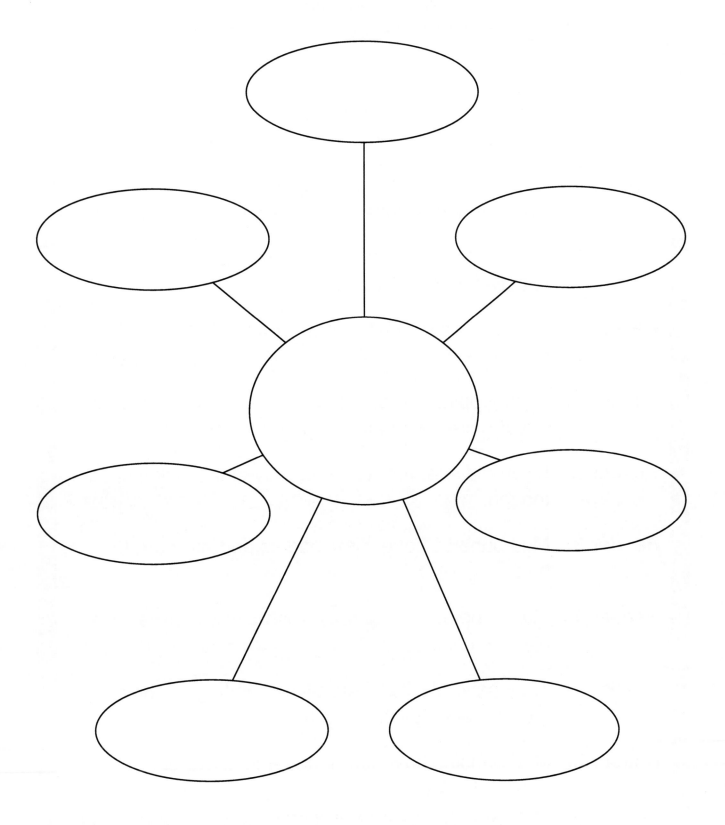

The Mud Puppy

BY CATHY DAVIS

A reader's theater with five parts

Reader 3: Would you like to learn about an unusual animal?

Reader 5: This animal has a scientific name, but most people call it a mud puppy or a waterdog.

Reader 1: It's not a dog at all, but it does live in the mud and water of ponds, lakes, and streams.

Reader 2: The mud puppy looks like a large salamander and is between 8 and 13 inches long.

Reader 4: You may have seen one as you waded in a stream.

Reader 1: Mud puppies are common in many states from the Great Lakes area all the way south to Georgia.

Reader 2: If you did see one, you probably didn't pick it up, though.

Reader 3: Mud puppies have slimy bodies and are hard to hold.

Reader 4: Mud puppies can be gray, rusty brown, or nearly black in color.

Reader 3: They have black or blue-black spotting on their backs and purplish-red gills.

Reader 5: Mud puppies have flat heads and short, but powerful tails.

The Mud Puppy *(cont.)*

Reader 1: Mud puppies will eat anything they can catch.

Reader 4: This includes insects, worms, fish, and salamanders.

Reader 3: But, their main food is crayfish.

Reader 2: Mud puppies must be careful because they have predators of their own.

Reader 5: Large fish are always hunting for mud puppies.

Reader 3: Mud puppies hide from their enemies under logs and rocks.

Reader 4: Their coloring gives them some protection from predators.

Reader 1: Mud puppies are not poisonous, but large ones may bite if bothered.

Reader 5: The female mud puppy carefully makes a nest cavity under stones or logs.

Reader 3: Then she lays up to 100 eggs in it and stays with the eggs until they hatch.

Reader 4: The mud puppy does not hibernate.

Reader 2: It remains active all through the year.

All: Mud puppy, mud puppy, down in the bog
Mud puppy, mud puppy, you old waterdog

Cool Cow Facts

CONNECTIONS

Literature Connection—*The Milk Makers* by Gail Gibbons

The Milk Makers uses colorful illustrations and diagrams to follow the path of milk from the cow to the supermarket.

Content Connections—Animals, Agriculture

Cool Cow Facts gives information about this important agricultural animal and helps the class to see the value of milk for their own developing bodies.

OBJECTIVE

Students will make, confirm, and revise simple predictions about what will be found in a text (e.g., uses prior knowledge and ideas presented in text, illustrations, titles, topic sentences, key words, and foreshadowing clues).

VOCABULARY

1. Introduce the key vocabulary words from the script. Write each word on the board.

2. Describe the meaning of each word and point out its use in the script.

3. Give students the opportunity to make physical connections with the vocabulary words. Have students make facial expressions, noises, and gestures to act out the words. For example, say to students, "Show me where on your body calcium is needed to make you strong."

   • **calcium**—a nutrient needed for strong bones and teeth

   • **calf**—a baby cow

   • **dairy**—having to do with milk and milk products

   • **Holstein**—black-and-white spotted cows that give milk

BEFORE THE READER'S THEATER

1. Read the title of the script and discuss the various roles. Then ask students to make predictions about the selection. What do they think this script will be about? Is it fiction or nonfiction? Why do they think so? Do they like milk? What are some other dairy products?

2. Read the script aloud, modeling appropriate reading strategies while you read. To help build fluency and comprehension, it is important for students to hear the script read aloud before practicing on their own.

Cool Cow Facts *(cont.)*

DURING THE READER'S THEATER

1. Divide the class into groups of six to read and practice the script.

2. Students need to decide which character they will play and then highlight their parts in the script (Readers 1–6). They should also mark with a star any places where they need to pause while reading.

3. Give students a few minutes to practice reading with expression in their voices. Additionally, students may decide on a few props or materials to use during their reading. They need to use materials that can be easily acquired or assembled in the classroom.

4. After they have finished practicing, have each group perform the reader's theater for the rest of the class. You may also want them to perform for another class. Students need to decide on their parts and then highlight them. They should also mark any places where they need to pause while reading.

AFTER THE READER'S THEATER

1. As a class, discuss the Semantic Map graphic organizer (page 72 or semanticmap.pdf). Have students copy the organizer. Have them refer back to the script to find the details necessary to complete the graphic organizer. Write *Dairy Cows* in the middle circle of the graphic organizer with main idea branches containing these words: *Milking, Milk, Cow's Diet*, and *Calves*. These are the main ideas about which students search for details to add under each heading.

2. Read other stories about cows and dairy farms. Encourage students to find both fiction and nonfiction books on the topic.

RESPONSE QUESTIONS

Group Discussion Questions

- Why might some children think that milk comes from a grocery store?

- Why do you think that milk is rushed so quickly to the store?

- Farmers put ID tags on each cow's ear so that they will know which cow is which. Why do you think the farmer would need to know that? Possible answer: The farmer keeps medical records on each cow just as a pediatrician does on each child. The farmer needs to keep track of which cows are due for vaccinations and which ones are on medication. He or she also needs to know how much milk a particular cow is producing. The farmer also keeps records of the cow's bloodline for breeding or selling purposes.

Written Response Question

- Do you think that it would be fun to work on a dairy farm? Why or why not?

Name _____ Date _____

Semantic Map

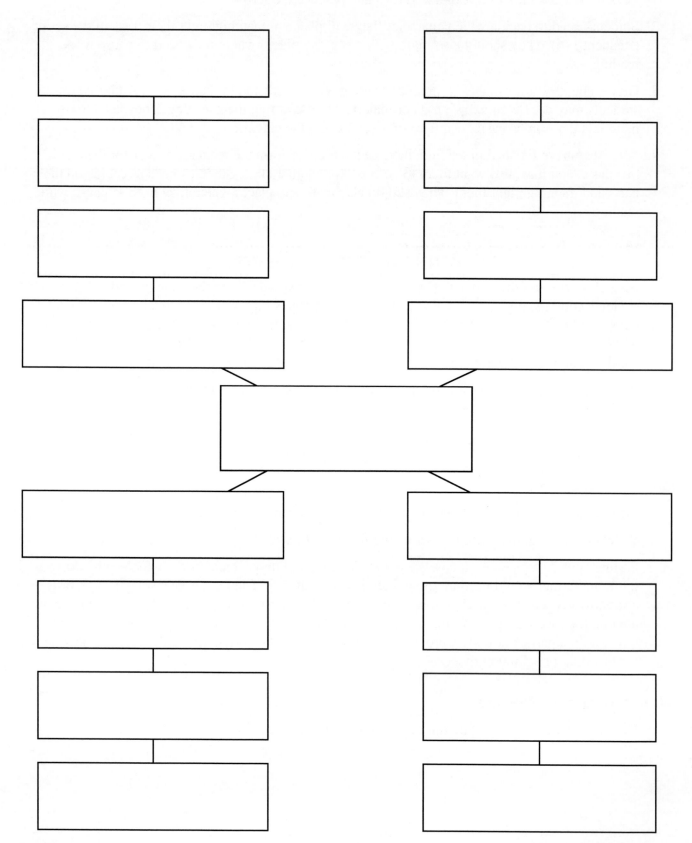

Cool Cow Facts

BY CATHY DAVIS

A reader's theater with six parts

Reader 1: Did you know that milk comes from healthy, well-fed dairy cows?

Reader 5: I bet some children think it comes from the dairy case at the grocery store!

Reader 2: Cows eat about 90 pounds of nutritious food a day.

Reader 4: That's more than most third graders weigh!

Reader 3: Cows spend about eight hours a day eating.

Reader 1: Can you imagine eating all day long?

Reader 2: They drink a lot, too.

Reader 3: Dairy cows drink nearly a bathtub full of water each day.

Reader 6: I heard that what a cow eats affects how much milk she makes.

Reader 5: A cow that eats only grass can make about 50 glasses of milk a day.

Reader 1: But a cow that eats grass, corn, hay, and mixed feed can make about 100 glasses of milk a day.

Cool Cow Facts *(cont.)*

Reader 4: That's enough for 30 children to have three glasses of milk a day!

Reader 6: Three servings of milk are what you need every day.

Reader 2: To get enough of an important thing called...

All: Calcium!

Reader 5: Your body needs calcium for strong bones and teeth.

Reader 1: What about chocolate milk? That's my favorite!

Reader 3: Chocolate milk is good for you, too, but it does have more sugar in it.

Reader 4: Farmers used to have to milk cows by hand.

Reader 3: It was slow work.

Reader 1: If you milked by hand, you could only milk about six cows an hour.

Reader 6: Using modern milking machines, farmers can milk 100 cows an hour.

Reader 4: The milk is cooled as soon as it leaves the cow.

Reader 3: In just two days, it's in a plastic jug at the grocery store, ready for your family to buy.

Cool Cow Facts *(cont.)*

Reader 6: From the cow to the store in two days?

Reader 4: And now for some interesting facts about cows:

Reader 2: All cows are females.

Reader 5: The males are called bulls.

Reader 1: Cows have four compartments in their stomachs.

All: We have just one.

Reader 4: Cows often have their ears pierced with I.D. tags.

Reader 2: This lets the dairy farmer know which cow is which.

Reader 4: A Holstein's black-and-white spots are like a fingerprint.

Reader 5: No two cows have exactly the same pattern of spots.

Reader 1: A cow must have a baby before she can produce milk.

Reader 6: It takes a cow nine months to have a baby, just like a human.

Reader 3: But a newborn calf is much larger than a human baby.

Reader 5: It weighs about 100 pounds when it is born.

Reader 2: It was fun learning about dairy cows.

Goldie and the Three Bears

CONNECTIONS

Literature Connection—*Goldilocks and the Three Bears* by James Marshall
Goldilocks and the Three Bears retells a familiar fairy tale with amusing pictures. A naughty Goldilocks learns her lesson when the bear family comes home.

Content Connections—Fairy Tales, Language Arts
Goldie and the Three Bears takes the basics of the original Goldilocks story and turns it on its head. Goldie is a pizza delivery boy and the bears are complete slobs! This script is a great introduction to a lesson on different versions of fairy tales from around the world.

OBJECTIVE

Students will understand similarities and differences within and among literary works from various genre and cultures (e.g., in terms of settings, character types, events, point of view; role of natural phenomena).

VOCABULARY

1. Introduce the key vocabulary words from the script. Write each word on the board.

2. Describe the meaning of each word and point out its use in the script.

3. Restate the definition or explanation of each vocabulary word. As you do, ask students to complete your statement by saying the vocabulary word. For example, say to students, "____ are delicious toppings for your pizza."

   • **anchovies**—small fish used in cooking and making sauces

   • **shock**—surprise

BEFORE THE READER'S THEATER

1. Read the title of the script and discuss the various roles. Then ask students to make predictions about the selection. What do they think this script will be about? Is it fiction or nonfiction? Why do they think so? What story does this script remind them of?

2. Tell students that as they read they should look for similarities and differences between this script and the Goldilocks story.

3. Read the script aloud, modeling appropriate reading strategies while you read. To help build fluency and comprehension, it is important for students to hear the script read aloud before practicing on their own.

Goldie and the Three Bears *(cont.)*

DURING THE READER'S THEATER

1. Divide the class into groups of seven to read and practice the script.

2. Students need to decide which character they will play and then highlight their parts in the script (Readers 1–3, Papa Bear, Goldie, Mama Bear, and Baby Bear). They should also mark with a star any places where they need to pause while reading.

3. Give students a few minutes to practice reading with expression in their voices. Additionally, students may decide on a few props or materials to use during their reading. They need to use materials that can be easily acquired or assembled in the classroom.

4. After they have finished practicing, have each group perform the reader's theater for the rest of the class. You may also want them to perform for another class.

AFTER THE READER'S THEATER

1. Display the Venn Diagram graphic organizer (page 78 or venndiagram.pdf). Help students compare the script with *Goldilocks and the Three Bears*. Record the similarities and differences in the graphic organizer.

2. Find other versions of *Goldilocks and the Three Bears* and read them to the class. There are many versions of this classic story. Discuss the differences and similarities among the versions.

RESPONSE QUESTIONS

Group Discussion Questions

- What did it mean that, "the family acted more like pigs"?

- What did Goldie mean when he said, "these cords are a bear to untangle"?

- What did Goldie mean at the end when he said, "business was booming"?

- What is the theme or big idea about this reading selection? (Suggested answers: helping others pays off, always do more than required and you will come out ahead, etc.)

Written Response Question

- Write about a time when you did something for someone else. How did it make you feel?

Name_____ Date _____

Venn Diagram

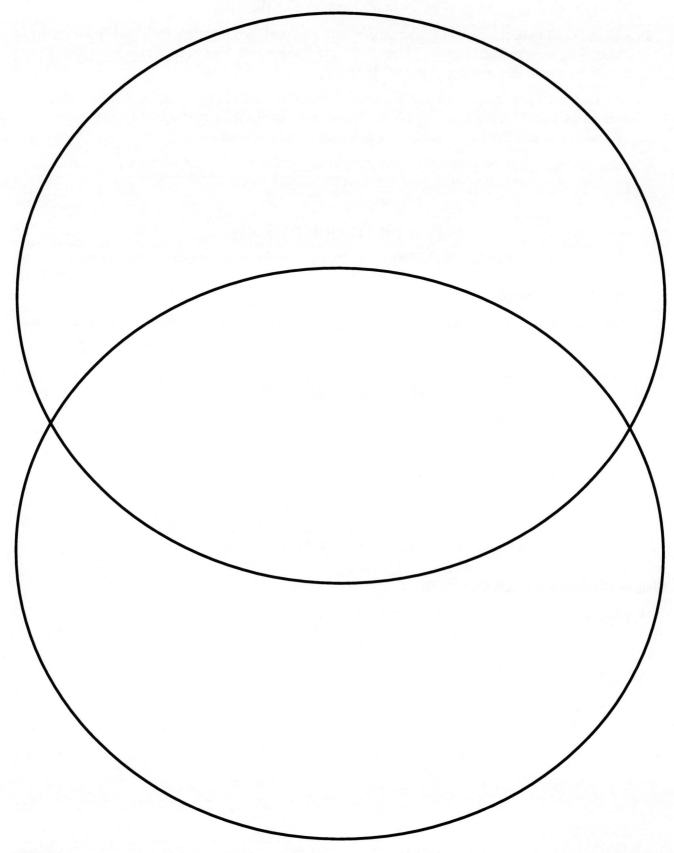

Goldie and the Three Bears

BY CATHY DAVIS

A reader's theater with seven parts

Reader 1: Once upon a time…

Reader 2: Sounds like a fairy tale to me.

Reader 1: There were three bears living deep in the forest.

Papa Bear: A papa bear!

Mama Bear: A mama bear!

Baby Bear: And baby bear with a teeny, tiny, squeaky voice!

Reader 3: Although they were bears, the family acted like slobs.

Reader 3: They weren't lazy, but they just didn't like housework.

Reader 1: It was their habit to take a stroll each morning while breakfast cooled.

Reader 2: Porridge, right?

Reader 1: No, pizza! I told you that this bear family was different.

Papa Bear: An extra large pizza supreme with anchovies for me!

Mama Bear: I want sausage, mushrooms, and peppers on mine.

Goldie and the Three Bears (cont.)

Baby Bear: Personal pan with cheese only is my favorite!

Papa Bear: Let's take a walk after Mama calls it in, and the food will be here when we get back.

Reader 1:   So the bears left their home and headed into the woods.

Reader 3:   Meanwhile, back at the house, the garbage cans were overflowing with empty pizza boxes.

Reader 2:   Dishes were piled up, and beds were not made.

Reader 3:   The den was covered with Papa's newspapers and Mama's knitting yarn.

Reader 1:   Scattered in front of the TV was a gigantic pile of Baby's video games, controllers, and tangled cords.

All: "Ding-dong," went the doorbell.

Reader 2:   Goldilocks, right?

Reader 1:   No. Standing on the front porch was Goldie, the pizza delivery boy.

Goldie: I guess no one is home. I'll just go on inside and wait for them to return. Someone needs to pay for these pizzas.

Reader 3:   Goldie pushed the door open and saw the mess. He couldn't believe his eyes!

Goldie and the Three Bears *(cont.)*

Goldie: These people live like pigs!

Reader 1:   And then Goldie had an idea.

Goldie: Maybe they'll give me a big tip if I straighten up this mess.

All: So Goldie began cleaning in a flurry.

Reader 3:   He took all of the dishes from the table to the sink, where he washed and scrubbed hardened pizza sauce and melted cheese until the plates were spotless.

Reader 1:   Then he wiped off the dining room table and reset it with the clean dishes.

Reader 2:   Then Goldie carried 25 empty pizza boxes outside to the garbage cans.

Goldie: Man it's tough getting these lids on because the cans are so full. Good thing today is garbage day. I bet this family hasn't set their trash out for weeks!

Reader 3:   So, Goldie rolled the cans out to the road and went back inside.

Goldie: That looks much better. I wonder what the other rooms look like.

Reader 3:   He started in the den. It took him quite a while to gather up Mama's knitting yarn and Papa's papers.

Goldie and the Three Bears (cont.)

Reader 2:	Then he stored the video games in the cabinet.
Reader 1:	But the tangled cords were another story.
Goldie:	What a mess! These cords are a bear to untangle! I might as well go upstairs and do the bedroom, too.
Reader 3:	By the time Goldie had made the beds, he was tired.
Goldie:	I think I'll just lie down on this small bed and rest.
Reader 2:	But before he knew it, Goldie was fast asleep.
Reader 1:	Meanwhile, the bear family had come back from their walk. They were standing in shock around the dining room table.
Papa Bear:	Someone has carried out all of the garbage!
Mama Bear:	Someone has washed all of the dishes!
Baby Bear:	Someone has delivered our pizzas! Let's eat!
Reader 3:	But instead of eating, the bears rushed into the den.
Mama Bear:	Someone has put my yarn into my knitting bag!
Baby Bear:	Someone has picked up my video controllers, and they even untangled the cords!
Reader 2:	About that time, Goldie let out a big snore.

Goldie and the Three Bears *(cont.)*

Papa Bear: What was that?

Reader 2: The bear family tiptoed up the stairs into the bedroom.

Papa Bear: Someone has made my bed!

Mama Bear: Someone has plumped up my pillows!

Baby Bear: Someone has tucked in my comforter, and that someone is still here!

Reader 1: Goldie opened his eyes to find the bears staring at him.

Reader 2: He screamed and ran out of the house, didn't he?

Reader 3: No, he opened his mouth and said…

Goldie: Hi, guys! Do you like what I did to your house?

Reader 2: The bears were so pleased with Goldie's work that they gave him an enormous tip.

Reader 1: It wasn't long before Goldie quit his pizza delivery job and started his own cleaning business.

Goldie: Business is booming! I'm making more money than I ever would have made at the pizza place.

All: So, this is one fairy tale with a happy ending for all.

Helping Monkeys

CONNECTIONS

Literature Connection—*Mom's Best Friend* by Sally Hobart Alexander

Mom's Best Friend tells the story of training a new guide dog for a blind person. It is based on Ms. Alexander's own experiences with blindness.

Content Connections—Animals, Science, Disabilities

Helping Monkeys is about monkeys trained to assist quadriplegic people. This script ties into units about individual differences.

OBJECTIVE

Students will summarize and paraphrase information in texts (e.g., includes the main idea and significant supporting details of a reading selection).

VOCABULARY

1. Introduce the key vocabulary words from the script. Write each word on the board.

2. Describe the meaning of each word and point out its use in the script.

3. Work together as a class to create a word web for each vocabulary word. Write the first vocabulary word in the center of a sheet of chart paper. Put a circle around the word. Then guide students in brainstorming related words, phrases, and examples to add to the web. Write students' responses around the vocabulary word and connect each one to the center circle in order to create a web. Post the word webs around the room for students' reference.

   - **depend**—to count on someone or something

   - **grateful**—thankful

   - **injured**—hurt

   - **paralyzed**—unable to move all or parts of your body

   - **quadriplegic**—a person who can't move both legs and both arms

BEFORE THE READER'S THEATER

1. Read the title of the script and discuss the various roles. Then ask students to make predictions about the selection. What do they think this script will be about? Is it fiction or nonfiction? Why do they think so? How could a monkey be a helper? What kinds of things could a monkey do?

2. Read the script aloud, modeling appropriate reading strategies while you read. To help build fluency and comprehension, it is important for students to hear the script read aloud before practicing on their own.

Helping Monkeys *(cont.)*

···

DURING THE READER'S THEATER
···

1. Divide the class into groups of five to read and practice the script. As they read they are to look for the main idea of the selection.

2. Students need to decide which character they will play and then highlight their parts in the script (Readers 1–5). They should also mark with a star any places where they need to pause while reading.

3. Give students a few minutes to practice reading with expression in their voices. Additionally, students may decide on a few props or materials to use during their reading. They need to use materials that can be easily acquired or assembled in the classroom.

4. After they have finished practicing, have each group perform the reader's theater for the rest of the class. You may also want them to perform for another class.

···

AFTER THE READER'S THEATER
···

1. As a class, complete the Main Idea and Details graphic organizer (page 86 or mainidea.pdf). The main idea that students should identify is that *monkeys can help quadriplegics*. Students should look through the script to add details to the graphic organizer.

2. Read other stories about animals that help people with disabilities. Encourage students to find both fiction and nonfiction books on the topic.

···

RESPONSE QUESTIONS
···

Group Discussion Questions

- Why wouldn't a seeing-eye dog be a good helper for a quadriplegic?

- Why do you think quadriplegics still need people to help them, even if they have a monkey helper?

- Why do you think that the organization that places the monkeys is called Helping Hands?

Written Response Question

- Would you like to be a foster parent to a baby monkey? Why or why not?

Name_____ Date _____

Main Idea and Details

Main Idea

Details

Details

Details

Details

Details

Helping Monkeys

BY CATHY DAVIS

A reader's theater with five parts

Reader 1: You have probably heard of seeing-eye dogs for the blind. But, did you know that monkeys also help disabled people?

Reader 3: People injured in car accidents, diving accidents, and falls sometimes lose control of their arms and legs.

Reader 5: These people are called quadriplegics.

Reader 2: Often times, quadriplegics have to depend on others.

Reader 3: They can't bathe, dress, or feed themselves without help.

Reader 4: Even with family, friends, or paid attendants, these people still spend many hours a day alone.

Reader 5: A doctor named Dr. Willard had the idea to train a small monkey to help one of her patients who was paralyzed.

Reader 2: She knew that her patient needed a helper who could be an extra pair of hands for him.

Reader 1: Today an organization called Helping Hands places monkey helpers with disabled people.

Reader 4: First the monkey lives with a human foster family for at least a year.

Reader 5: Caring for a baby monkey is hard work.

Helping Monkeys *(cont.)*

Reader 4: The foster parents pay the vet bills and provide a cage six feet high.

Reader 3: They take care of the baby monkey as if it were a child.

Reader 2: The foster parents feed the monkey, play with it, and change its diapers.

Reader 5: Then the family teaches the monkey to do many things while it lives with them.

Reader 2: The monkey learns to turn lights on and off on command.

Reader 4: It also learns how to open the refrigerator and bring snacks to people.

Reader 3: It picks up things dropped on the floor.

Reader 5: The monkey even learns to get water and put a straw into the cup.

Reader 3: The total cost of breeding, training, and placing a monkey helper is $25,000.

Reader 1: But the monkey may live to help a disabled person for many years.

All: So, it's worth the price!

Reader 5: Many quadriplegic people are grateful for their monkey helpers.

Chickenpox

CONNECTIONS

Literature Connection—*Herbie Jones Reader's Theater* by Suzy Kline

"Herbie and Annabelle" from *Herbie Jones Reader's Theater* is a fictional script about finding friends in unexpected places. Herbie and Annabelle don't usually get along. However, things change after Herbie is drafted by his teacher to deliver the class cards to Annabelle when she is at home with the chickenpox.

Content Connections—Health, Science

Chickenpox teaches about a virus that still affects many young children. Students will have a better understanding of what chickenpox involves if they read this script before the literature selection.

OBJECTIVE

Students will summarize and paraphrase information in texts (e.g., includes the main idea and significant supporting details of a reading selection).

VOCABULARY

1. Introduce the key vocabulary words from the script. Write each word on the board.

2. Describe the meaning of each word and point out its use in the script.

3. Write the following cloze sentences on the board: An ____ person can pass an illness to another person; The doctor examined my ____ when my tummy hurt; Fever and a sore throat are ____ of strep throat; The common cold is easy to catch. It is ____ to others; We planted a row of ____ in the garden; A ____ must run its course. Antibiotics do not cure it. Have students take turns coming to the board and choosing the correct word for each of the following sentences.

   - **abdomen**—the area of the body that contains the stomach
   - **chickpeas**—a plant grown for its short pods and seeds
   - **contagious**—can catch by contact
   - **infected**—carrying germs for a disease
   - **symptoms**—physical disturbance that is evidence of a disease
   - **virus**—a microscopic agent that causes contagious disease

BEFORE THE READER'S THEATER

1. Read the title of the script and discuss the various roles. Then ask students to make predictions about the selection. What do they think this script will be about? Is it fiction or nonfiction? Why do they think so? Ask if anyone has ever had chickenpox or seen anyone with chickenpox?

2. Read the script aloud, modeling appropriate reading strategies while you read. To help build fluency and comprehension, it is important for students to hear the script read aloud before practicing on their own.

Chickenpox (cont.)

BEFORE THE READER'S THEATER (cont.)

3. Display the Cluster Map graphic organizer (page 91 or clustermap.pdf) and write *Chickenpox* in the center of it. Tell students to look for the main ideas in the script as they read it.

DURING THE READER'S THEATER

1. Divide the class into groups of five to read and practice the script.

2. Students need to decide which character they will play and then highlight their parts in the script (Readers 1–5). They should also mark with a star any places where they need to pause while reading.

3. Give students a few minutes to practice reading with expression in their voices. Additionally, students may decide on a few props or materials to use during their reading. They need to use materials that can be easily acquired or assembled in the classroom.

4. After they have finished practicing, have each group perform the reader's theater for the rest of the class. You may also want them to perform for another class.

AFTER THE READER'S THEATER

1. As a class, complete the Cluster Map graphic organizer. Help students find the main ideas about chickenpox for the headings in the organizer. (Hint: Have students look at the last line in the script.)

2. Headings for the graphic organizer should include the following: *Chickenpox* (in the center of the cluster map), *Treatment, Symptoms,* and *Prevention* (in the three large circles outside of the center). After the main headings are added to the organizer, students should brainstorm details from the script to add under each heading.

3. Have students write a letter to a family member explaining what they learned about chickenpox.

RESPONSE QUESTION

Group Discussion Questions

- What is the main thing that bothers people with chickenpox?

- How could an infected person pass the disease on to others and not know it?

- What are two reasons that a person with chickenpox should not scratch? How would trimming your fingernails help?

- Why might a person with chickenpox not want hot or spicy foods?

- What do you think is the author's purpose of the "All" parts? (Suggested answer: to add some humor or to give a feeling to the reader of what chickenpox is like)

Written Response Question

- If you were visiting a friend who had chickenpox, what are some things that you could do to help the friend to keep his or her mind off the itching?

Name_____ Date _____

Cluster Map

Chickenpox

BY CATHY DAVIS

A reader's theater with five parts

Reader 1: No one knows for certain how chickenpox got its name.

Reader 4: We do know that the disease has nothing to do with chickens.

Reader 2: Perhaps the red spots were once thought to look like chickpeas on the skin.

Reader 5: Chickenpox is a disease caused by a virus.

Reader 1: Although anyone of any age can get it, it's more common in children under the age of 15.

Reader 3: Chickenpox is highly contagious. This means that you can easily catch it, if exposed to an infected person.

Reader 5: It is so contagious that if someone in your household has chickenpox, nearly all of the family members who haven't had the disease will get it.

Reader 4: A cough or a sneeze can send droplets containing the virus through the air.

Reader 2: Or you can get it from direct contact with an infected person.

Reader 1: You can come down with chickenpox for up to 21 days after being exposed to it.

Chickenpox *(cont.)*

Reader 4: If you have chickenpox, you're contagious before you know that you have it.

Reader 3: You might infect others and not even realize that you're sick.

Reader 5: Your first symptoms are often a slight fever, runny nose, or cough.

Reader 4: You may not want to eat very much.

Reader 1: You may complain of a headache or feel tired.

Reader 2: In other words, you just don't feel well, but you don't know what's wrong.

Reader 5: The rash begins, and after a few days, it's obvious that you have chickenpox.

Reader 3: Small red bumps usually appear on your face, back, or abdomen first.

Reader 1: The rash keeps spreading more each day.

Reader 5: The red bumps develop into itchy blisters.

Reader 3: The blisters later break open, leaving sores.

Reader 5: You should stay home from school until all of the blisters have dried up.

Chickenpox (cont.)

Reader 1: This usually takes a week to 10 days.

Reader 4: Treatment can only help you to feel more comfortable while the disease runs its course.

Reader 2: The rash itches and makes you want to scratch.

Reader 3: But if you do, you may cause scars or infection.

Reader 1: Trim your fingernails.

Reader 4: Take several oatmeal baths to relieve the itching.

Reader 5: Put lotion on the itchy areas.

All: I know I can't scratch, but I want to so badly. Chickenpox, I hate it madly.

Reader 2: Luckily, most people only have chickenpox once.

Reader 3: Since 1995, a vaccine has been given to prevent this disease, but it's not 100% effective.

Reader 5: Some people who receive the vaccination will still get chickenpox.

Reader 1: But they usually have a much milder case and a faster recovery.

Reader 4: Now you know about the symptoms, treatment, and prevention of chickenpox.

The Charreada

CONNECTIONS

Literature Connection—*Anthony Reynoso: Born to Rope* by Martha Cooper and Ginger Gordon

Anthony Reynoso: Born to Rope is a nonfiction selection and photographic essay about a Mexican American boy and a skill passed down through his family—exhibition roping.

Content Connections—Mexico, Hispanic Themes, Social Studies

The Charreada tells about the rich cultural tradition of Mexico's national sport—the Mexican rodeo. This script will fit into any lesson about Mexico, its people, and its history.

OBJECTIVE

Students will summarize and paraphrase information in texts (e.g., includes the main idea and significant supporting details of a reading selection).

VOCABULARY

1. Introduce the key vocabulary words from the script. Write each word on the board.

2. Describe the meaning of each word and point out its use in the script.

3. Use cloze sentences to solidify students' understanding of the vocabulary words. On a sheet of chart paper, write a cloze sentence for each vocabulary word. Chorally read the first cloze sentence. Ask students to talk with a partner to determine which vocabulary word correctly completes the sentence. After students identify the correct word, write it in the blank on the chart paper. Repeat this process for the remaining cloze sentences.

   - **competition**—a contest
   - **culture**—a group of people's way of life
   - **gallop**—the gait when a horse runs
   - **sidesaddle**—when the rider puts both legs on the same side of the horse
   - **sombrero**—wide-brimmed hat

BEFORE THE READER'S THEATER

1. Read the title of the script and discuss the various roles. Then ask students to make predictions about the selection. What do they think this script will be about? Is it fiction or nonfiction? Why do they think so? What is a charreada? Do they think it is an English word?

2. Introduce the Concept Web graphic organizer (page 97 or conceptweb.pdf). Write the word *rodeo* in the center and ask students to brainstorm associated words for the rest of the web. Has anyone been to a rodeo? Display another copy of the Concept Web graphic organizer and write the word *charreada* in the center. Tell students to watch for key words to complete the web while they read.

The Charreada (cont.)

BEFORE THE READER'S THEATER (cont.)

3. Read the script aloud, modeling appropriate reading strategies while you read. To help build fluency and comprehension, it is important for students to hear the script read aloud before practicing on their own.

DURING THE READER'S THEATER

1. Divide the class into groups of five to read and practice the script.

2. Students need to decide which character they will play and then highlight their parts in the script (Readers 1–5). They should also mark with a star any places where they need to pause while reading.

3. Give students a few minutes to practice reading with expression in their voices. Additionally, students may decide on a few props or materials to use during their reading. They need to use materials that can be easily acquired or assembled in the classroom.

4. After they have finished practicing, have each group perform the reader's theater for the rest of the class. You may also want them to perform for another class.

AFTER THE READER'S THEATER

1. As a class, select key words from the script to complete the Concept Web graphic organizer.

2. Read other stories about Mexico. Encourage students to find both fiction and nonfiction books on the topic.

RESPONSE QUESTIONS

Group Discussion Questions

- What does "tailing the bull" mean?
- What are the rules in bull riding and wild mare riding?
- What does the charro wear?
- How does the community get involved?

Written Response Question

- Would you like to see a charreada? Why or why not?

Name_____ Date _____

Concept Web

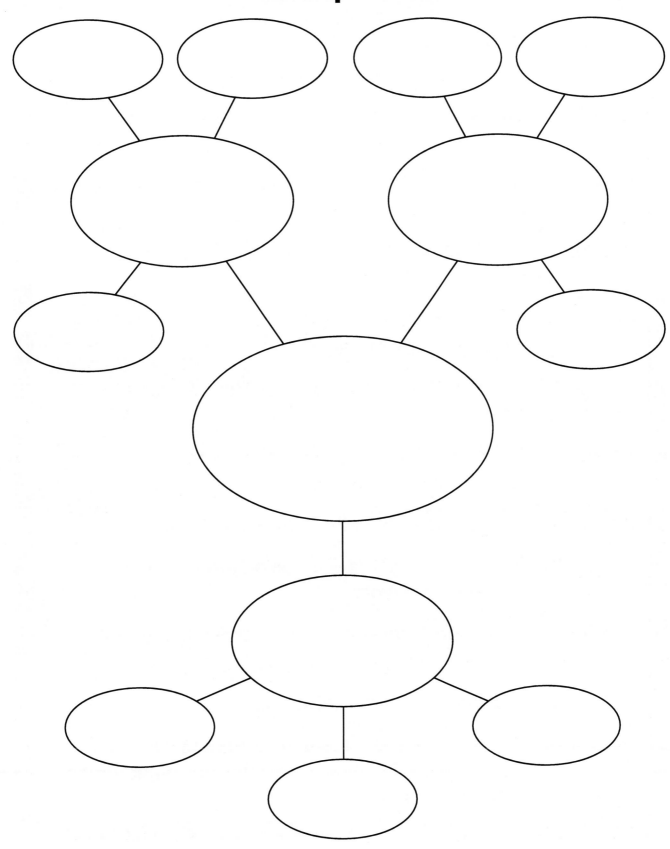

The Charreada

BY CATHY DAVIS

A reader's theater with five parts

Reader 2: El Charro means "man on horseback" in Spanish.

Reader 5: This is the Mexican version of the American cowboy.

Reader 1: But the Mexican cowboy has been around a lot longer.

Reader 4: The Spanish were the first to bring horses and cattle to Mexico.

Reader 3: Contests began on these ranches to show off the cowboys' skills of roping and riding.

Reader 1: This is how the charreada, or Mexican rodeo, started.

Reader 3: The charreada is a source of pride for Mexicans and Mexican Americans.

Reader 5: It's a celebration of the Mexican culture.

Reader 2: Four hundred years of tradition are part of the nine scored events.

Reader 1: Unlike the American rodeo, teamwork and skill usually count more than speed.

Reader 2: One event is called "tailing the bull."

Reader 3: In this competition, the charro rides his horse alongside a wild bull and reaches down and grabs the bull by the tail.

The Charreada *(cont.)*

Reader 4: Then he flips the bull over onto its back.

Reader 1: Bull riding and wild mare riding are two other scored events.

Reader 2: The rules are the same in both of them.

Reader 5: The charros rides until the animal stops bucking or until they fall off, whichever happens first.

Reader 4: One of the most colorful parts of the Mexican rodeo is called Escaramuza.

Reader 3: Teams of girls dressed in traditional costumes ride sidesaddle and gallop and crisscross in dangerous patterns.

Reader 2: The men competing wear neckties or large bow ties, spurred boots, tight riding pants, and short jackets.

Reader 5: A wide-brimmed sombrero with ribbon decorations and braids complete the outfit.

Reader 3: When the charreada has ended, the Mexican community gathers for an evening of food, dancing, and visiting.

Reader 3: Many people, on both sides of the border, enjoy the charreada.

References Cited

Kuhn, Melanie R. and Steven A. Stahl. 2000. *Fluency: A review of developmental and remedial practices*. Ann Arbor, MI: Center for the Improvement of Early Reading Achievement.

LaBerge, David and S. Jay Samuels. 1974. Toward a theory of automatic information processing in reading. *Cognitive Psychology* 6: 293–323.

National Reading Panel. 2000. *Teaching children to read: An evidence-based assessment of the scientific research literature on reading and its implications for reading instruction—reports of the subgroups*. Washington, DC: National Institute of Child Health and Human Development.

Rasinski, Timothy. 1990. *The effects of cued phrase boundaries in texts*. Bloomington, IN: ERIC Clearinghouse on Reading and Communication Skills.

Samuels, S. Jay. 1979. The method of repeated reading. *The Reading Teacher* 32: 403–408.

U.S. Department of Education. 2001. *Put Reading First: The Research Building Blocks for Teaching Children to Read*. Washington, DC: U.S. Government Printing Office.

Recommended Children's Literature

Alexander, Sally Hobart. *Mom's Best Friend*. New York: Simon and Schuster, 1992.

Barber, Barbara. *Allie's Basketball Dream*. New York: Lee & Low Books, 1998.

Bradby, Marie. *More Than Anything Else*. New York: Scholastic, 1995.

Brenner, Barbara and Julia Takaya. *Chibi: A True Story from Japan*. Mooloolaba QLD, Australia: Sandpiper, 1999.

Christelow, Eileen. *What Do Authors Do?* New York: Clarion Books, 1997.

Cooper, Martha and Ginger Gordon. *Anthony Reynoso: Born to Rope*. New York: Clarion Books, 1996.

Friedrich, Elizabeth. *Leah's Pony*. Honesdale, PA: Boyds Mills Press, 1999.

Gibbons, Gail. *The Milk Makers*. New York: Atheneum, 1985.

Jenkins, Martin. *Fly Traps! Plants that Bite Back*. Sommerville, MA: Candlewick, 1996.

Kline, Suzy. *Herbie Jones Reader's Theater*. New York: Penguins Young Readers Group, 1997.

Marshall, James. *Goldilocks and the Three Bears*. London: Puffin Books, 1998.

Pinkwater, Daniel. *Guys from Space*. New York: Aladdin, 1992.

Scott, Ann Herbert. *Brave as a Mountain Lion*. New York: Clarion Books, 1996.

Teague, Mark. *How I Spent My Summer Vacation*. New York: Dragonfly Books, 1997.

Contents of the
Teacher Resource CD

Script Title	Filename
Booker T. Washington	bookertwashington.pdf
The Rhyming Author	rhymingauthor.pdf
Black Bart the Po8	blackbart.pdf
The Radio Show that Frightened Thousands	radioshow.pdf
The Dust Bowl	dustbowl.pdf
The Story of Basketball	storyofbasketball.pdf
The Mountain Lion	mountainlion.pdf
Learn About Ducks	learnaboutducks.pdf
The Mud Puppy	mudpuppy.pdf
Cool Cow Facts	coolcowfacts.pdf
Goldie and the Three Bears	goldie.pdf
Helping Monkeys	helpingmonkeys.pdf
Chickenpox	chickenpox.pdf
The Charreada	charreada.pdf
Graphic Organizer	**Filename**
Summary Pyramid	summarypyramid.pdf
K-W-L Chart	kwlchart.pdf
Box Summary	boxsummary.pdf
Question Strips	questionstrips.pdf
Main Idea and Details	mainideaanddetails.pdf
Story Map	storymap.pdf
Information Web	informationweb.pdf
Main Idea and Details Web	mainideaweb.pdf
Brainstorm Web	brainstormweb.pdf
Semantic Map	semanticmap.pdf
Venn Diagram	venndiagram.pdf
Main Idea and Details	mainidea.pdf
Cluster Map	clustermap.pdf
Concept Web	conceptweb.pdf

Notes

Notes